AF688502

AI Wealth Revolution

AI Wealth Revolution

Matthew Petchinsky

1

AI Wealth Revolution: Unlocking the Trillionaire Mindset
By: Matthew Petchinsky

Introduction

The Age of AI Wealth

In the past few decades, the world has witnessed seismic shifts in how wealth is created, distributed, and accumulated. From the industrial revolution to the information age, each epoch has brought about new opportunities for those ready to harness its potential. Today, we stand on the cusp of the next great transformation: the age of artificial intelligence (AI). Unlike previous revolutions, AI is not merely a tool or a single industry—it is a catalyst that is reshaping every facet of human life and business.

AI has already demonstrated its potential to revolutionize industries. In healthcare, AI algorithms analyze medical data with unparalleled speed and accuracy, saving lives while cutting costs. In finance, AI-driven platforms manage investments, forecast market trends, and execute trades in milliseconds, outperforming human capabilities. E-commerce giants like Amazon leverage AI to predict customer preferences, optimize supply chains, and even develop new products. Creative industries, once thought impervious to automation, now benefit from AI tools capable of generating art, composing music, and writing books.

But this is just the beginning. Experts estimate that AI will contribute over $15 trillion to the global economy by 2030. The rise of AI is not just about improving efficiency or creating new conveniences; it is about unlocking unprecedented levels of wealth. For those who understand how to harness its power, the opportunities are limitless. Becoming an AI trillionaire is not a pipe dream—it is the inevitable outcome for those who think big, act strategically, and adapt quickly.

As AI becomes increasingly accessible, it levels the playing field. No longer is cutting-edge technology reserved for large corporations or tech-savvy entrepreneurs. Today, anyone with vision and determination can tap into AI's potential to create, innovate, and amass wealth. This book is your guide to understanding how AI can help you achieve financial independence and beyond, breaking down barriers to entry and equipping you with the tools to ride the wave of this economic revolution.

The Trillionaire's Blueprint

Achieving unparalleled wealth in the age of AI requires more than just understanding the technology—it demands a complete shift in mindset. To join the ranks of the world's wealthiest individuals, you must adopt what this book refers to as the "trillionaire mindset." This mindset is a blend of vision, strategy, adaptability, and relentless curiosity.

1. **Vision**: The foundation of the trillionaire mindset is the ability to see beyond the present. It's about identifying not just what AI can do today but imagining what it will enable tomorrow. A visionary approach means thinking long-term and spotting opportunities before they become obvious.
2. **Strategy**: Vision without action is merely a dream. A trillionaire mindset includes the ability to develop actionable strategies to turn ideas into reality. This involves leveraging AI to optimize decision-making, automate processes, and scale operations. It's about working smarter, not harder.
3. **Adaptability**: In an AI-driven world, change is constant. Technologies evolve, industries shift, and new competitors emerge seemingly overnight. The ability to pivot, learn new skills, and embrace uncertainty is crucial for staying ahead of the curve. Trillionaires are not afraid of failure—they see it as a stepping stone to success.
4. **Curiosity**: At the heart of innovation lies curiosity. The trillionaire mindset thrives on asking questions, exploring possibilities, and challenging the status quo. By staying curious and open to new ideas, you can uncover hidden opportunities and drive groundbreaking innovations.

This book will not only teach you how to leverage AI for wealth creation but also how to cultivate the mindset needed to capitalize on this era of unprecedented opportunity. It's a blueprint for anyone ready to embrace AI as the ultimate tool for financial freedom and generational wealth.

Whether you're an entrepreneur looking to disrupt an industry, an investor seeking the next big opportunity, or a creative mind eager to monetize your talents, this book will provide the insights and strategies you need. The age of AI wealth is here. The only question is: will you seize the opportunity or watch it pass you by?

Prepare to explore a world where AI is not just a tool but a partner in your journey to becoming a trillionaire. Let's begin.

Part 1: Understanding AI Wealth Potential

Chapter 1: The AI Economy: A Billion-Dollar Foundation

Introduction to the AI Economy

The global economy is undergoing a transformation driven by artificial intelligence (AI). No longer a futuristic concept confined to science fiction, AI is now a cornerstone of innovation, reshaping industries and unlocking wealth on an unprecedented scale. In 2023 alone, the global AI market was valued at approximately $200 billion, and projections indicate it will surpass $1 trillion by 2030. The AI economy is not a single sector but a dynamic ecosystem encompassing industries, technologies, and applications that collectively redefine how wealth is created, distributed, and sustained.

This chapter provides an overview of AI's impact on global wealth creation, exploring its foundational role in various industries, its capacity to drive efficiency and innovation, and its potential to democratize access to opportunities. From healthcare to manufacturing, from finance to entertainment, AI is the engine powering the next great economic revolution.

The Economic Pillars of AI

1. Productivity and Efficiency

AI's primary contribution to the economy lies in its ability to enhance productivity and efficiency. Through automation, machine learning, and advanced data analysis, AI enables businesses to achieve more with less:

- **Automation of Repetitive Tasks**: AI-powered robots and software can handle mundane, time-consuming tasks, freeing up human resources for higher-value activities. For example, in manufacturing, AI-driven robotics optimize assembly lines, reducing errors and increasing production speed.
- **Predictive Analytics**: AI systems analyze vast datasets to identify patterns and trends, helping businesses anticipate customer needs, optimize supply chains, and reduce waste. Companies like Amazon and Walmart have leveraged AI to streamline operations, saving billions annually.

2. Innovation and New Market Creation

AI is not just about improving existing systems—it also creates entirely new markets and industries:

- **AI-Driven Technologies**: Innovations like autonomous vehicles, personalized healthcare, and generative AI are spawning billion-dollar industries. For example, the self-driving car market alone is projected to reach $62 billion by 2030.
- **Transformative Products and Services**: AI-powered apps, such as language translation tools, virtual assistants, and recommendation engines, redefine consumer experiences and generate new revenue streams.

3. Democratization of Opportunities

AI's accessibility is leveling the playing field for entrepreneurs, startups, and small businesses:

- **Low-Cost AI Tools**: Platforms like OpenAI's ChatGPT, Google's AI Suite, and Microsoft Azure AI provide affordable solutions for individuals and businesses to harness AI's power.
- **Global Reach**: AI-driven digital platforms enable businesses to operate globally, connecting with customers, suppliers, and partners across borders with minimal barriers.

AI's Impact Across Key Industries

1. Healthcare

The healthcare sector is experiencing a paradigm shift thanks to AI:

- **Early Diagnosis and Precision Medicine**: AI algorithms analyze medical images, genetic data, and patient records to detect diseases earlier and recommend personalized treatments. Companies like DeepMind and IBM Watson Health have made significant advancements in these areas.
- **Operational Efficiency**: AI-powered scheduling, resource allocation, and patient monitoring reduce hospital costs and improve patient outcomes.

2. Finance

The financial sector is one of the earliest adopters of AI, leveraging its capabilities to maximize profits and minimize risks:

- **Algorithmic Trading**: AI systems process market data in real-time, executing trades with precision and speed, often outperforming human traders.
- **Fraud Detection**: AI analyzes transactional data to identify unusual patterns, protecting consumers and institutions from fraudulent activities.
- **Personalized Financial Planning**: Robo-advisors like Betterment and Wealthfront use AI to offer tailored investment strategies.

3. Retail and E-Commerce

AI has transformed how we shop:

- **Personalized Shopping Experiences**: AI algorithms predict consumer preferences, recommend products, and create seamless online shopping experiences.
- **Inventory Management**: Retailers use AI to forecast demand, optimize inventory levels, and reduce waste.

4. Entertainment and Media

AI is redefining content creation and consumption:

- **Content Generation**: AI tools like DALL-E and ChatGPT create music, art, and writing, enabling rapid production of creative content.
- **Audience Targeting**: Streaming platforms like Netflix and Spotify use AI to personalize recommendations, keeping users engaged and driving revenue.

5. Manufacturing and Logistics
AI enhances operational efficiency and drives innovation in production:

- **Smart Factories**: AI-powered machinery improves precision and reduces production costs.
- **Supply Chain Optimization**: AI predicts demand, identifies bottlenecks, and ensures timely deliveries.

Economic Ripple Effects of AI

1. Job Creation and Transformation

Contrary to fears of mass unemployment, AI is creating new job opportunities:

- **AI Development Roles**: Positions in AI engineering, data science, and machine learning are in high demand.
- **Complementary Careers**: AI's integration into industries creates roles in oversight, training, and enhancement of AI systems.

2. Wealth Redistribution

AI enables wealth creation for individuals and communities previously excluded from economic growth:

- **Remote Work Opportunities**: AI-powered platforms facilitate remote entrepreneurship and gig work, empowering individuals in underrepresented regions.
- **Microbusiness Expansion**: Small businesses can scale globally by leveraging AI for marketing, operations, and customer engagement.

Challenges and Considerations

While the AI economy offers tremendous opportunities, it also presents challenges that must be addressed:

- **Ethical Concerns**: Issues surrounding data privacy, bias, and AI misuse must be tackled to ensure equitable growth.
- **Skill Gaps**: As AI reshapes industries, workforce retraining and education are critical to prevent economic disparities.
- **Regulatory Frameworks**: Governments must establish regulations that balance innovation with consumer protection.

Conclusion

The AI economy is not a distant possibility—it is here, transforming industries, creating new markets, and redefining how wealth is built and sustained. Those who understand its potential and act strategically will be positioned to thrive in this new era. By leveraging AI's power to drive productivity, foster innovation, and democratize opportunities, you can become a key player in this billion-dollar foundation and potentially scale your ambitions to the trillion-dollar mark. The future belongs to those who seize it, and AI is the key to unlocking unprecedented prosperity.

Chapter 2: Mindset Mastery: Thinking Like an AI Trillionaire

Introduction to the Trillionaire Mindset

The path to becoming an AI trillionaire starts not with technology but with your mindset. The difference between those who merely use AI and those who leverage it to create monumental wealth lies in their approach to thinking, problem-solving, and vision. A trillionaire mindset is not about having all the answers—it's about asking the right questions, seeing opportunities where others see obstacles, and committing to continuous growth and innovation.

In this chapter, we'll explore the key principles of developing a mindset primed for success in the AI-driven world. You'll learn how to adopt the mental frameworks of the world's most successful entrepreneurs, innovators, and visionaries, empowering you to think strategically, adapt rapidly, and seize opportunities as they arise.

1. The Foundation of Visionary Thinking

To leverage AI effectively, you must first cultivate visionary thinking. This involves looking beyond the present and imagining the possibilities of the future. Visionary thinkers operate on three key principles:

- **Seeing the Bigger Picture**: Trillionaires understand that AI is not just a tool but a transformative force that can revolutionize entire industries. They constantly ask, "What's next?" and anticipate where technology will lead.
- **Thinking in Systems**: Rather than focusing on isolated problems, think of how systems interconnect. AI thrives on data, relationships, and feedback loops. Learn to identify how one innovation can ripple through multiple sectors.
- **Challenging Assumptions**: Visionary thinkers don't take the status quo for granted. They question existing norms and imagine better ways to solve problems or create value.

2. Developing Strategic Foresight

Strategic foresight is the ability to anticipate future trends, identify opportunities, and act on them. In the age of AI, this skill is invaluable. Here's how to hone it:

- **Stay Informed**: Continuously educate yourself about AI advancements, emerging markets, and global economic shifts. Use tools like AI news aggregators and industry reports to stay ahead of the curve.
- **Spot Patterns**: Train your mind to recognize patterns in data, behaviors, and market trends. AI excels at pattern recognition, and by learning to think similarly, you can better predict opportunities.
- **Scenario Planning**: Imagine different future scenarios based on current trends. Consider how AI could disrupt industries or create new needs, and position yourself to capitalize on these changes.

3. Embracing a Growth Mindset

A growth mindset is the belief that your abilities and intelligence can be developed through dedication and hard work. This mindset is critical for navigating the rapidly changing AI landscape.

- **Learn from Failure**: AI innovation often involves trial and error. Adopt a perspective that views failures as valuable learning experiences rather than setbacks.
- **Seek Feedback**: Surround yourself with advisors, mentors, and peers who can provide constructive criticism and fresh perspectives. AI thrives on feedback loops; apply this principle to your personal and professional growth.
- **Stay Curious**: Cultivate a sense of wonder and curiosity about the world. Ask questions, explore new fields, and embrace lifelong learning.

4. Cultivating Boldness and Risk-Taking

The biggest rewards come to those willing to take calculated risks. To think like an AI trillionaire, you must develop the courage to make bold moves while managing potential downsides.

- **Experiment Freely**: Use AI to test ideas quickly and at a low cost. Whether it's launching a new product, analyzing a market, or prototyping a solution, AI allows for rapid iteration and learning.
- **Make Data-Driven Decisions**: Balance boldness with informed decision-making. Leverage AI's analytical capabilities to evaluate risks and predict outcomes, minimizing uncertainty.
- **Adopt a Long-Term Perspective**: Trillionaires think in decades, not months. Focus on building sustainable wealth and innovation rather than chasing short-term gains.

5. Building an Adaptable and Resilient Mindset

AI's rapid evolution means that adaptability is essential. A trillionaire mindset embraces change and thrives under uncertainty.

- **Stay Agile**: Be ready to pivot when circumstances change. AI can provide real-time insights that help you adapt your strategies quickly.
- **Practice Resilience**: Success often comes after multiple failures. Develop mental toughness and a positive outlook to keep pushing forward despite setbacks.
- **Welcome Disruption**: View disruptions as opportunities to innovate. When AI upends an industry, ask yourself, "How can I lead the way in this new landscape?"

6. Thinking Exponentially

One of the most powerful aspects of AI is its ability to scale exponentially. Trillionaire thinkers understand this principle and apply it to their strategies.

- **Leverage AI's Scalability**: Use AI to automate processes, replicate solutions, and reach global audiences with minimal additional cost.
- **Focus on Multipliers**: Identify opportunities where AI can amplify your efforts. For example, AI-driven marketing can exponentially increase customer engagement and sales.
- **Build Ecosystems, Not Products**: Think beyond individual offerings. Create interconnected systems where each component reinforces the others, maximizing value.

7. Harnessing Emotional Intelligence

AI may excel at processing data, but human connection remains critical. A trillionaire mindset blends technological prowess with emotional intelligence to inspire teams, build relationships, and create meaningful impact.

- **Lead with Empathy**: Understand the needs and aspirations of your customers, employees, and stakeholders. Use AI tools to gather insights while maintaining a human touch.
- **Communicate Effectively**: Articulate your vision clearly and inspire others to join you. AI can assist in tailoring communication strategies to different audiences.
- **Foster Collaboration**: Use AI to facilitate teamwork and innovation, breaking down silos and encouraging cross-disciplinary partnerships.

Conclusion: Becoming the Architect of Your Future

Developing a trillionaire mindset is not about adopting a single way of thinking—it's about embracing a comprehensive approach that combines vision, strategy, adaptability, and emotional intelligence. In the AI-driven world, wealth creation is no longer limited by traditional barriers. With the right mindset, you can harness AI to unlock limitless opportunities, transform industries, and create a legacy of innovation and impact.

As you move forward in this book, remember that your mindset is your most valuable tool. AI can provide the data, tools, and insights, but it's your ability to think strategically, act decisively, and dream boldly that will set you apart. With the foundations of a trillionaire mindset, you are not just keeping pace with the future—you are shaping it.

Chapter 3: The AI Tools You Need to Know

Introduction to AI Tools

Artificial Intelligence (AI) has evolved into a vast ecosystem of tools, platforms, and applications designed to empower individuals and businesses to accomplish tasks more efficiently, scale operations, and unlock new levels of innovation. Whether you're an entrepreneur, investor, artist, or simply someone looking to improve productivity, understanding the essential AI tools available is crucial. These tools not only simplify complex tasks but also open doors to opportunities previously thought unattainable.

This chapter provides an in-depth guide to the most impactful AI tools across various domains, categorized by their primary uses. You'll learn what these tools are, how they function, and how they can be leveraged to build wealth and achieve your goals.

1. AI for Content Creation

1.1 Writing and Editing

- **ChatGPT by OpenAI**: A natural language processing tool that generates text based on prompts, ideal for writing blogs, scripts, books, or even brainstorming ideas.
  - **Use Case**: Quickly draft and edit high-quality content for websites, newsletters, or books.
- **Grammarly**: An AI-powered grammar and style checker that ensures professional and polished writing.
  - **Use Case**: Enhance writing quality and consistency across professional communications.
- **Jasper AI**: A tool tailored for marketers and creators to generate ad copy, blog posts, and social media content.
  - **Use Case**: Save time creating optimized, audience-specific content.

1.2 Visual Content

- **DALL·E**: An image generation tool that creates visuals from text prompts, ideal for marketing and creative projects.
  - **Use Case**: Design unique artwork, product visuals, or illustrations for books and campaigns.
- **Canva AI**: Combines AI with intuitive design tools to create presentations, social media posts, and branded visuals.
  - **Use Case**: Streamline graphic design for non-designers.
- **Runway**: A platform for generating and editing videos with AI, offering features like background removal and video synthesis.
  - **Use Case**: Produce professional-grade videos without the need for advanced editing skills.

2. AI for Business and Productivity
2.1 Automation

- **Zapier**: Connects apps and automates workflows, reducing manual tasks and improving efficiency.
  - **Use Case**: Automate repetitive tasks like sending emails, updating spreadsheets, or syncing data between platforms.
- **UiPath**: A robotic process automation (RPA) tool that automates business processes across industries.
  - **Use Case**: Implement end-to-end automation for complex workflows.

2.2 Project Management

- **Notion AI**: Enhances productivity by integrating AI into task management, brainstorming, and document creation.
  - **Use Case**: Streamline project planning and collaboration.
- **Asana with AI**: A project management tool with AI features that prioritize tasks and offer predictive insights.
  - **Use Case**: Keep projects on track and anticipate potential delays.

2.3 Virtual Assistants

- **Siri, Alexa, and Google Assistant**: AI-powered voice assistants that perform tasks such as scheduling, reminders, and controlling smart devices.
  - **Use Case**: Manage day-to-day tasks hands-free.

3. AI for Financial Management and Investment
3.1 Personal Finance

- **Mint AI**: Offers budget tracking and personalized financial advice.
  - **Use Case**: Gain control over personal spending and savings goals.
- **YNAB (You Need A Budget)**: Uses AI to help users create and stick to a budget.
  - **Use Case**: Maximize savings through data-driven budgeting.

3.2 Investment Tools

- **Robo-Advisors (Betterment, Wealthfront)**: AI-driven investment platforms that optimize portfolios based on user preferences and risk tolerance.
  - **Use Case**: Automate investments with low fees and consistent rebalancing.
- **Trade Ideas**: A stock market AI platform that provides real-time trading alerts and strategies.
  - **Use Case**: Identify high-potential trades in stock markets.

4. AI for Marketing and Sales
4.1 Email Marketing

- **Mailchimp with AI**: Automates email marketing campaigns with AI-generated subject lines and personalized content recommendations.
  - **Use Case**: Increase email engagement and conversions.
- **HubSpot AI**: Provides marketing automation tools for lead generation, customer tracking, and campaign optimization.
  - **Use Case**: Streamline customer acquisition and retention.

4.2 Social Media Management

- **Hootsuite Insights**: Uses AI to analyze social media trends and optimize posting strategies.
  - **Use Case**: Maximize social media reach and engagement.
- **Lately AI**: Automatically generates social media posts based on long-form content like blogs or videos.
  - **Use Case**: Save time on content repurposing while maintaining brand consistency.

5. AI for Creative Industries
5.1 Music Creation

- **AIVA**: An AI composer that creates original music for videos, games, and personal projects.
  - **Use Case**: Generate royalty-free music tailored to your needs.
- **Amper Music**: Allows users to compose soundtracks by selecting mood, genre, and instrumentation.
  - **Use Case**: Enhance multimedia projects with custom soundtracks.

5.2 Game Development

- **Unity ML-Agents**: AI tools for game developers to create intelligent in-game behaviors.
  - **Use Case**: Build immersive, AI-driven gaming experiences.
- **Artbreeder**: Generates unique character designs and environments for gaming or storytelling.
  - **Use Case**: Rapidly prototype visual elements for creative projects.

6. AI for Learning and Skill Development
6.1 Personalized Learning Platforms

- **Duolingo with AI**: Adapts language learning to the user's progress and challenges.
  - **Use Case**: Master a new language efficiently.
- **Khan Academy AI**: Provides tailored educational content and feedback powered by AI.
  - **Use Case**: Accelerate learning in a wide range of subjects.

6.2 AI Code Assistants

- **GitHub Copilot**: Assists developers by suggesting code snippets and debugging solutions.
  - **Use Case**: Speed up software development and reduce errors.
- **DeepCode**: An AI-powered code review tool.
  - **Use Case**: Improve the quality and security of your code.

7. AI for Data Analysis and Research
7.1 Business Intelligence

- **Tableau with AI**: Offers data visualization and predictive analytics.
  - **Use Case**: Turn raw data into actionable insights.
- **Google Analytics 360**: Uses AI to analyze website traffic and customer behavior.
  - **Use Case**: Optimize digital marketing strategies.

7.2 Research Tools

- **Semantic Scholar**: An AI-powered research tool for academic articles.
  - **Use Case**: Quickly find relevant studies and papers.
- **Quillbot**: Simplifies complex information and assists in summarizing research.
  - **Use Case**: Save time when processing large amounts of text.

Conclusion: Choosing the Right Tools

With the extensive range of AI tools available, the key to success lies in selecting the ones that align with your goals. Start small, experiment with different platforms, and integrate tools that provide the highest value for your needs. Whether you aim to write a bestseller, launch a business, or optimize your finances, there is an AI tool designed to help you achieve your vision.

Remember, these tools are only as powerful as the person using them. By combining a strong mindset with the right AI resources, you can unlock unlimited possibilities and step into the age of AI-driven wealth creation.

Chapter 4: Building Your AI-Powered Network

Introduction: The Power of an AI-Powered Network

In today's interconnected world, success is no longer a solo journey. Building and nurturing a strong network is vital for personal and professional growth. However, in the age of artificial intelligence, the nature of networking has evolved. AI has transformed how we connect, collaborate, and build relationships, offering tools and platforms that amplify our ability to grow and maintain a powerful network.

This chapter explores how you can leverage AI to build an AI-powered network that not only supports your goals but also scales with your ambitions. You'll learn about the tools, strategies, and mindset required to harness AI for meaningful collaboration, smarter networking, and exponential growth.

1. Understanding the AI-Powered Network

An AI-powered network is more than a collection of contacts—it's an ecosystem of relationships enhanced and managed through AI tools and strategies. This network maximizes efficiency, enhances collaboration, and opens up opportunities that might otherwise be missed.

- **Key Features of an AI-Powered Network**:
  - **Personalization**: AI analyzes data to tailor your interactions and engagement.
  - **Scalability**: Automation allows you to maintain connections at scale.
  - **Insights**: AI-driven analytics provide insights into the strength and potential of your relationships.
  - **Proactivity**: AI tools can anticipate needs, suggest connections, and automate follow-ups.

2. Tools for Building an AI-Powered Network

2.1 Networking Platforms

- **LinkedIn with AI**:
  - AI tools on LinkedIn suggest connections based on your industry, skills, and goals.
  - **Use Case**: Build a professional network by connecting with thought leaders and collaborators.
- **Shapr**:
  - A networking app that uses AI to match you with like-minded professionals.
  - **Use Case**: Discover new connections in your field or area of interest.
- **Lunchclub**:
  - An AI-powered platform that facilitates one-on-one networking meetings.
  - **Use Case**: Forge deep connections with individuals tailored to your goals.

2.2 AI for Communication

- **Grammarly and ChatGPT**:
  - Enhance your communication with AI-assisted writing tools for emails, pitches, and follow-ups.
  - **Use Case**: Ensure your messaging is professional and impactful.
- **Crystal**:
  - An AI tool that analyzes personalities and suggests tailored communication strategies.
  - **Use Case**: Approach each connection with a personalized tone and style.

2.3 CRM and Relationship Management

- **HubSpot CRM with AI**:
  - Automates customer relationship management, offering insights and reminders for follow-ups.
  - **Use Case**: Manage professional relationships effectively without losing track of key details.
- **Affinity**:
  - A relationship intelligence platform that tracks and strengthens your network.
  - **Use Case**: Prioritize high-value connections and opportunities.

2.4 Collaboration Tools

- **Slack with AI**:
  - Facilitates communication and collaboration within teams, with AI-driven reminders and insights.
  - **Use Case**: Streamline project discussions and maintain team engagement.
- **Zoom AI**:
  - Offers automated transcription, action item summaries, and scheduling features.
  - **Use Case**: Enhance remote meetings and ensure follow-through on collaborative tasks.

3. Strategies for AI-Enhanced Networking

3.1 Automating the Connection Process

- Use AI tools to automate repetitive tasks such as sending connection requests, personalized messages, and follow-ups.
- **Example**: LinkedIn's AI-generated messages can introduce you to new contacts while maintaining a personal touch.

3.2 Identifying High-Value Connections

- AI tools like Affinity and LinkedIn's Premium features provide analytics to identify which connections are most valuable to your goals.
- Prioritize these relationships by offering value and staying engaged.

3.3 Leveraging AI to Find Opportunities

- AI-powered platforms like AngelList and Meetup suggest events, partnerships, and projects based on your interests and expertise.
- **Example**: Use Meetup to discover local or virtual networking events tailored to your industry.

3.4 Enhancing Collaboration Through AI

- Encourage the use of collaborative AI tools within your network, such as shared CRM systems, cloud-based workspaces, and project management platforms.
- Build trust by sharing resources and knowledge facilitated through AI.

4. Building Authentic Relationships in an AI-Driven World

While AI can streamline networking, the foundation of meaningful relationships remains authenticity. Here's how to balance AI efficiency with genuine human connection:

4.1 Personalize Every Interaction

- Use AI to gather insights but ensure your interactions are thoughtful and sincere.
- **Example**: Before a meeting, use Crystal to understand someone's communication preferences, but engage in a natural and unscripted conversation.

4.2 Offer Value First

- AI tools can help identify ways to add value to your connections, whether through introductions, resources, or advice.
- **Example**: Use LinkedIn to share relevant articles or congratulate someone on their achievements.

4.3 Follow-Up with Care

- Automate reminders with tools like HubSpot, but ensure your follow-ups are timely and relevant.
- **Example**: After a networking event, send a personalized message referencing your conversation.

5. Scaling Your AI-Powered Network

5.1 Expanding Beyond Borders

- AI makes it easier than ever to build a global network. Use platforms like Zoom and LinkedIn to connect with individuals worldwide.
- Collaborate across time zones with scheduling tools like Calendly.

5.2 Creating Online Communities

- Use AI tools like Discord bots or Facebook's AI group management features to create and manage online communities.
- **Example**: Start a niche group for professionals in your field and use AI to moderate discussions and suggest relevant topics.

5.3 Maintaining Relationships at Scale

- With tools like Nimble and Salesforce Einstein, manage hundreds or even thousands of relationships without sacrificing depth.

6. Overcoming Challenges in AI-Powered Networking

- **Data Privacy**: Always respect privacy laws and ethical standards when using AI tools to gather insights.
- **Over-Automation**: Avoid making your interactions feel robotic or impersonal; balance AI with genuine human engagement.
- **Platform Fatigue**: Focus on a few key tools rather than spreading yourself too thin across multiple platforms.

Conclusion: Your Network is Your Net Worth

In the age of AI, the adage "your network is your net worth" has never been truer. By leveraging AI tools and strategies, you can build a network that supports your ambitions, provides value to others, and scales with your vision.

The tools and techniques outlined in this chapter are the foundation for creating an AI-powered network that not only enhances your professional life but also drives exponential growth in opportunities and success. The key lies in combining AI's efficiency with the authenticity of genuine relationships, ensuring that your network is not just vast but also deeply meaningful.

Part 2: AI in Content Creation

Chapter 5: AI and Publishing: Becoming a Bestseller

Introduction: The Age of AI in Publishing

The publishing industry has undergone a radical transformation in recent years, and at the heart of this revolution is artificial intelligence (AI). From conceptualizing ideas to marketing finished works, AI has become an indispensable tool for authors and publishers. Whether you're an aspiring writer or a seasoned publisher, understanding how to harness AI in every stage of the book creation and marketing process can help you not only produce high-quality books but also position them to become bestsellers.

This chapter explores how AI can assist in writing, editing, designing, and marketing your books. By leveraging AI tools and strategies, you can streamline the publishing process, reach broader audiences, and maximize sales potential.

1. Writing with AI

AI has made writing more accessible and efficient than ever. With the right tools, you can generate ideas, structure your book, and produce high-quality content in a fraction of the time it would traditionally take.

1.1 Idea Generation and Outlining

- **AI Tools for Brainstorming**:
  - Tools like **ChatGPT** and **Sudowrite** help generate fresh ideas, expand on concepts, and outline chapters.
  - **Use Case**: Enter a prompt like "Generate 10 unique ideas for a fantasy novel" to explore creative directions.
- **Mind Mapping with AI**:
  - Tools like **Coggle** and **MindMeister** use AI to help visually organize ideas into coherent structures.

1.2 Writing and Drafting

- **AI-Assisted Writing Platforms**:
  - Platforms like **Jasper AI** and **Writesonic** can help draft chapters, expand paragraphs, or create vivid descriptions.
  - **Use Case**: Write a draft faster by collaborating with AI to flesh out scenes, dialogue, or technical details.
- **Overcoming Writer's Block**:
  - AI tools suggest next lines, offer plot twists, or reframe existing text to keep your creativity flowing.

1.3 Research Assistance

- **Semantic Scholar** and **Perplexity AI** provide access to academic articles, data, and resources to enrich your writing with accurate details.
- **Use Case**: Integrate real-world facts or historical context into your book without spending hours on research.

2. Editing with AI

Editing is often the most time-intensive part of publishing, but AI has revolutionized the process, offering tools to streamline and enhance the editing phase.

2.1 Grammar and Style

- **Grammarly**: AI-powered grammar, punctuation, and style checker.
    - **Use Case**: Ensure your manuscript is polished and professional.
- **ProWritingAid**: Combines grammar correction with deeper insights into sentence structure, pacing, and word choice.
    - **Use Case**: Optimize the readability and flow of your writing.

2.2 Structural Editing

- **Autocrit**: Focuses on structural elements like pacing, genre-specific conventions, and overused words.
    - **Use Case**: Tailor your book to meet the expectations of your target audience.
- **Fictionary**: Provides a visual analysis of story arcs, character development, and plot progression.
    - **Use Case**: Identify and fix inconsistencies in your story structure.

2.3 Beta Reading with AI

- **Natural Language AI**: Offers feedback by analyzing your manuscript from a reader's perspective, highlighting areas for improvement.
    - **Use Case**: Get a sense of how your target audience might respond to your work.

3. Designing Your Book with AI

The cover design, layout, and overall presentation of your book significantly impact its success. AI tools make professional-grade design accessible to all authors.

3.1 Cover Design

- **Canva AI**: Create stunning book covers with customizable templates and AI-assisted design recommendations.
    - **Use Case**: Develop an eye-catching cover that aligns with your genre and target audience.
- **Book Brush**: A tool specifically for authors to design covers, 3D mockups, and promotional images.
    - **Use Case**: Generate professional-quality visuals for marketing.

3.2 Interior Formatting

- **Atticus.io**: An AI-driven tool for formatting manuscripts into professional layouts for print and eBooks.
    - **Use Case**: Easily format your manuscript for multiple publishing platforms.
- **Vellum**: Specializes in formatting for eBooks and print with minimal technical effort.
    - **Use Case**: Ensure your book looks polished on every device.

4. Marketing Your Book with AI

Creating a great book is only half the battle. AI excels in helping authors identify their target audience, craft effective marketing campaigns, and optimize sales strategies.

4.1 Identifying Your Audience

- **Facebook Audience Insights**: Uses AI to analyze audience demographics, interests, and behaviors.
    - **Use Case**: Target ads to the right readers based on data.
- **Helium 10**: Helps identify profitable keywords and market trends for self-published authors on Amazon.
    - **Use Case**: Optimize your book's metadata to improve discoverability.

4.2 Social Media Marketing

- **Buffer with AI**: Automates social media posts and analyzes engagement to optimize your online presence.
    - **Use Case**: Schedule posts and track performance across multiple platforms.
- **Lately AI**: Repurposes long-form content into social media posts.
    - **Use Case**: Turn excerpts from your book into engaging tweets, posts, or reels.

4.3 Email Marketing

- **Mailchimp AI**: Automates email campaigns with AI-generated subject lines and personalized recommendations.
    - **Use Case**: Build a mailing list and nurture relationships with your readers.

4.4 Ads and Promotions

- **Amazon Advertising**: AI-driven tools for creating targeted ad campaigns within the Kindle ecosystem.
    - **Use Case**: Increase your book's visibility among Amazon's vast reader base.
- **Google Ads with AI**: Optimizes ad targeting and budgets for promoting your book across the web.
    - **Use Case**: Drive traffic to your website or online store.

5. Self-Publishing Platforms Powered by AI

5.1 Amazon Kindle Direct Publishing (KDP)

- Use Amazon's AI tools for keyword optimization, pricing strategies, and sales tracking.
- **Use Case**: Maximize sales on the world's largest eBook marketplace.

5.2 Draft2Digital

- Distributes your book to multiple platforms while offering AI-driven formatting and marketing tools.
- **Use Case**: Expand your reach to Apple Books, Barnes & Noble, and more.

5.3 IngramSpark

- Offers print-on-demand services with AI tools for market analysis.
- **Use Case**: Publish high-quality physical books without upfront inventory costs.

6. AI-Enhanced Analytics for Success

Understanding what works and what doesn't is critical for long-term success. AI provides powerful tools for analyzing sales performance, reader behavior, and market trends.

- **Amazon Author Central**: Offers data on sales, rankings, and reviews.
- **Google Analytics**: Tracks website traffic, helping you understand how readers discover and interact with your content.
- **BookStat**: Provides sales and revenue data across multiple platforms in real-time.

7. Overcoming Challenges with AI in Publishing

7.1 Maintaining Authenticity

- AI can assist, but it's your unique voice that will resonate with readers. Use AI as a tool, not a replacement for creativity.

7.2 Avoiding Overreliance

- Diversify your strategies. While AI is powerful, combining it with traditional methods can lead to greater success.

7.3 Ethical Considerations

- Ensure transparency if using AI-generated content and avoid plagiarism or excessive automation that diminishes quality.

Conclusion: AI as Your Publishing Ally

The tools and strategies outlined in this chapter can transform how you approach the publishing process, enabling you to write, edit, design, and market books with greater efficiency and impact. By leveraging AI, you not only streamline your workflow but also increase your chances of creating a bestseller.

In the age of AI, publishing success is no longer limited by time, resources, or expertise. With the right mindset and tools, you can turn your creative vision into a thriving career, reaching readers around the globe and establishing yourself as a bestselling author in the AI-powered era.

Chapter 6: Creating Viral Content with AI

Introduction: The Power of Viral Content

In the digital age, viral content is the gold standard for capturing attention, building an audience, and driving engagement. Whether it's a trending blog post, an attention-grabbing video, or a share-worthy social media post, viral content has the potential to skyrocket your brand, product, or message to a global audience. The challenge, however, lies in consistently creating high-quality content that resonates deeply with your audience.

This is where artificial intelligence (AI) becomes a game-changer. AI tools can help you generate ideas, optimize your messaging, and even predict what content is most likely to go viral. In this chapter, we'll explore how to leverage AI for crafting video scripts, blogs, and social media posts that have the potential to captivate audiences and achieve viral success.

1. Understanding Viral Content

Before diving into AI tools, it's essential to understand the components of viral content. Viral content typically shares the following characteristics:

- **Emotional Resonance**: Content that evokes strong emotions (e.g., joy, anger, awe) is more likely to be shared.
- **Relatability**: Content that speaks to shared experiences or challenges connects with a broader audience.
- **Novelty**: Unique, surprising, or creative content grabs attention.
- **Utility**: Informative or helpful content encourages sharing for its value.

AI tools can help you identify these elements and integrate them into your content creation process.

2. Leveraging AI for Video Scripts

Videos are one of the most engaging forms of content on the internet. From YouTube tutorials to TikTok reels, the right video can gain millions of views in a matter of hours. AI can streamline the process of creating compelling video scripts.

2.1 Generating Ideas for Video Content

- **ChatGPT**: Generate a list of video ideas based on your niche or target audience.
    - **Example**: For a fitness brand, prompt ChatGPT with "Generate 10 viral video ideas for a fitness YouTube channel."
- **AnswerThePublic**: An AI tool that reveals trending questions and topics people are searching for in your niche.

2.2 Writing Engaging Scripts

- **Jasper AI**: Use this tool to write polished video scripts tailored to your audience.
    - **Example**: Enter a prompt like "Write a YouTube script for a motivational video about overcoming failure."
- **Writesonic**: Offers specific templates for different video types, including tutorials, product reviews, and inspirational content.

2.3 Enhancing Video Content with AI Tools

- **Synthesia**: Create AI-driven videos with realistic avatars and voiceovers, saving time and production costs.
    - **Use Case**: Produce professional explainer videos or tutorials without hiring actors or voiceover artists.
- **Pictory**: Automatically generates videos from your text content, complete with visuals and voiceovers.
    - **Use Case**: Turn blog posts or articles into short, engaging video summaries.

3. Crafting Blogs That Go Viral with AI

Blogs remain a powerful medium for thought leadership, storytelling, and SEO-driven traffic. With AI, you can create highly engaging, shareable blog content that resonates with your audience.

3.1 Topic Research

- **BuzzSumo**: Analyze trending topics and identify content that performs well in your industry.
    - **Use Case**: Discover which subjects are most likely to attract attention and shares.
- **Frase.io**: Uses AI to suggest blog topics based on popular keywords and questions.
    - **Use Case**: Identify gaps in existing content to create blogs that fill those needs.

3.2 Writing High-Quality Blogs

- **ChatGPT**: Write complete blog drafts or expand on existing ideas.
    - **Example**: Prompt ChatGPT with "Write a 1,000-word blog post on the benefits of mindfulness in the workplace."
- **Surfer SEO**: Combines AI with SEO insights to optimize your blog for search engines.
    - **Use Case**: Ensure your content ranks well by targeting the right keywords and formatting.

3.3 Optimizing Readability and Engagement

- **Hemingway Editor**: Uses AI to simplify complex sentences and improve readability.
    - **Use Case**: Make your content more accessible to a broader audience.
- **Grammarly**: Ensures your blogs are grammatically correct and stylistically polished.

4. Creating Viral Social Media Posts with AI

Social media is the heartbeat of viral content. AI can help you craft posts that resonate with your audience, time them perfectly, and analyze their performance for future improvement.

4.1 Writing Captivating Social Media Posts

- **Jasper AI Social Templates**: Offers pre-made templates for Facebook, Twitter, Instagram, and LinkedIn posts.
    - **Use Case**: Create attention-grabbing headlines, hashtags, and captions.
- **Lately AI**: Automatically generates social media posts from long-form content like blogs or videos.
    - **Use Case**: Repurpose content across multiple platforms to maximize engagement.

4.2 Optimizing Timing and Reach

- **Buffer**: An AI-powered tool for scheduling posts and analyzing engagement data.
    - **Use Case**: Post at the optimal times for your audience to maximize reach.
- **Hootsuite Insights**: Uses AI to track trends and suggest posting times and formats.

4.3 Creating Visual Content for Social Media

- **Canva AI**: Generate eye-catching visuals and graphics tailored to each platform.
    - **Use Case**: Design Instagram carousel posts or Pinterest pins with ease.
- **DALL·E**: Generate unique images to accompany your posts, making them stand out in crowded feeds.

4.4 Using AI for Hashtag and Trend Analysis

- **RiteTag**: Suggests the best hashtags for your posts based on content and audience.
    - **Use Case**: Increase the visibility of your posts with targeted hashtags.
- **TrendSpottr**: Identifies trending topics and hashtags in real-time.
    - **Use Case**: Stay ahead of social media trends and align your content with what's popular.

5. Analyzing and Iterating with AI

Creating viral content is not just about producing great material—it's about understanding what works and improving over time.

5.1 Performance Analytics

- **Google Analytics**: Tracks the performance of your blogs and social media referrals.
- **Socialbakers**: Provides detailed insights into engagement metrics across platforms.

5.2 A/B Testing

- Use AI tools like **Optimizely** to test different versions of your content.
    - **Use Case**: Determine which headlines, images, or formats perform best.

5.3 Sentiment Analysis

- **MonkeyLearn**: Analyzes audience reactions to your content for sentiment (positive, negative, neutral).
    - **Use Case**: Adjust your tone and messaging to better align with your audience's preferences.

6. Strategies for Viral Success

6.1 Hook Your Audience Early

- Use AI tools to craft compelling introductions or headlines that immediately grab attention.
    - **Example**: Jasper AI can generate multiple headline variations for A/B testing.

6.2 Leverage Emotional Triggers

- AI sentiment analysis tools like MonkeyLearn can help identify which emotional triggers resonate most with your audience.

6.3 Collaborate with Influencers

- Use AI platforms like **Upfluence** to identify influencers in your niche.
    - **Use Case**: Partner with individuals who can amplify your content.

6.4 Repurpose Content Across Platforms

- AI tools like Lately AI and Pictory make it easy to adapt your content for different formats, increasing its potential reach.

Conclusion: AI as Your Content Creation Ally

In the digital world, creating viral content is both an art and a science. AI tools offer you the scientific precision needed to optimize ideas, scripts, blogs, and social media posts for maximum impact. By combining these tools with your creativity, you can consistently produce content that captivates audiences, builds your brand, and drives engagement.

The strategies and tools outlined in this chapter are not just about going viral—they're about creating meaningful connections and delivering value to your audience. When used effectively, AI can turn content creation from a time-consuming challenge into a powerful, results-driven process.

Chapter 7: Music and Art: Crafting Creative Empires

Introduction: The Creative Revolution Powered by AI

The arts, once seen as a realm solely dominated by human creativity, have been transformed by artificial intelligence (AI). With the rise of AI-driven tools, composing music, generating art, and building creative empires is no longer limited to those with formal training or years of experience. These technologies have democratized creative industries, allowing anyone with a vision to bring their ideas to life.

This chapter explores how AI tools are empowering creators to compose original music, generate stunning art, and establish creative empires that transcend traditional boundaries. Whether you're a musician, visual artist, or entrepreneur seeking to monetize creative content, the integration of AI into your workflow can amplify your capabilities, streamline production, and open new avenues for revenue.

1. AI in Music Composition

AI is revolutionizing the way music is created, from ideation to production. Tools that analyze patterns in sound, suggest chord progressions, and even compose entire pieces are now accessible to anyone.

1.1 AI-Powered Composition Tools

- **AIVA (Artificial Intelligence Virtual Artist)**:
  - Composes original music in various styles, such as classical, pop, and cinematic.
  - **Use Case**: Create soundtracks for films, video games, or advertising campaigns.
- **Amper Music**:
  - Allows users to compose custom music by selecting mood, style, and instrumentation.
  - **Use Case**: Enhance videos, podcasts, or presentations with original music.
- **Soundraw**:
  - Generates royalty-free music tracks tailored to specific genres and themes.
  - **Use Case**: Produce background music for YouTube or social media content.

1.2 Music Production with AI Tools

- **LANDR**:
  - An AI-driven platform for mastering tracks, optimizing audio quality for professional results.
  - **Use Case**: Polish your music before releasing it on streaming platforms.
- **Endlesss**:
  - A collaborative music creation app powered by AI that enables real-time jamming with others.
  - **Use Case**: Co-create music with artists worldwide.

1.3 Enhancing Creativity in Music

- **Google Magenta**:
  - Uses machine learning to create new musical compositions and experiment with unique sounds.
  - **Use Case**: Break creative blocks by exploring unconventional melodies and rhythms.
- **Melody Assistant**:
  - Suggests harmonies, counterpoints, and variations to enrich compositions.
  - **Use Case**: Refine and expand your musical ideas.

2. AI in Visual Arts

AI is not only enhancing traditional art forms but also enabling the creation of entirely new ones. From digital paintings to 3D models, AI-driven tools allow artists to explore uncharted creative territories.

2.1 Generative Art Tools

- **DALL·E by OpenAI**:
  - Generates unique, high-quality images based on text prompts.
  - **Use Case**: Create custom visuals for marketing, book covers, or personal projects.
- **Runway**:
  - A platform for generating and editing images, videos, and other multimedia using AI.
  - **Use Case**: Develop visual content for advertising campaigns or social media.
- **Artbreeder**:
  - Allows users to create and customize portraits, landscapes, and abstract art using AI.
  - **Use Case**: Design characters or settings for storytelling or game development.

2.2 AI for Animation and Video

- **DeepMotion**:
  - Uses AI to convert static images or designs into animations.
  - **Use Case**: Create dynamic marketing videos or animated short films.
- **Pictory**:
  - Generates video content from scripts or blog posts, complete with visuals and voiceovers.
  - **Use Case**: Repurpose written content into engaging video formats.

2.3 Enhancing Traditional Art with AI

- **Adobe Sensei**:
  - Integrates AI into Adobe's suite of tools, offering features like content-aware fills and intelligent resizing.
  - **Use Case**: Streamline photo editing, graphic design, and digital painting workflows.
- **Procreate with AI Plugins**:
  - AI-enhanced tools for iPad artists, providing brush customization, color suggestions, and effects.
  - **Use Case**: Elevate your digital illustrations with AI-powered assistance.

3. Monetizing AI-Generated Music and Art

While AI simplifies the creative process, building a sustainable empire requires strategic monetization. Here are ways to profit from AI-generated music and art:

3.1 Selling Music and Soundtracks

- **Stock Music Platforms**:
  - Upload AI-generated tracks to platforms like AudioJungle or Pond5 for passive income.
- **Streaming Services**:
  - Distribute music through platforms like Spotify and Apple Music using services like DistroKid.
- **Custom Compositions**:
  - Offer bespoke music creation services for brands, filmmakers, or content creators.

3.2 Selling Art

- **Print-on-Demand Services**:
  - Platforms like Printful or Redbubble allow you to sell AI-generated art as prints, clothing, or merchandise.
- **NFTs (Non-Fungible Tokens)**:
  - Mint and sell unique digital artworks as NFTs on platforms like OpenSea or Rarible.
- **Stock Image Sites**:
  - Upload visuals to sites like Shutterstock or Adobe Stock for passive income.

3.3 Licensing Creative Assets

- License your AI-generated music or art for use in advertisements, video games, or films.

4. AI Tools for Building a Creative Brand

Establishing a recognizable brand is key to growing a creative empire. AI tools can streamline branding and audience engagement:

4.1 Social Media Presence

- **Hootsuite with AI**:
  - Schedules and optimizes social media posts for maximum reach.
  - **Use Case**: Promote your music or art effectively across platforms.
- **Canva AI**:
  - Design cohesive branding materials like logos, banners, and social media graphics.

4.2 Website Creation

- **Wix ADI**:
  - Uses AI to design professional websites tailored to your needs.
  - **Use Case**: Showcase your portfolio and provide a platform for direct sales.

4.3 Audience Insights

- **Google Analytics**:
  - Tracks visitor behavior on your website, helping you refine your content strategy.
  - **Use Case**: Understand what resonates with your audience to improve engagement.

5. Collaborating with AI for Continuous Growth

AI is not just a tool but a creative partner that can grow with you. Here's how to maximize its potential:

5.1 Experimentation

- Use AI tools to explore styles, genres, and mediums you wouldn't normally consider.
  - **Example**: Combine classical music elements with modern electronic beats using AIVA.

5.2 Community Building

- Share AI-generated creations on platforms like Behance or SoundCloud to build a following.
- Collaborate with other creators using AI-driven platforms like Endlesss for music or DeviantArt for visuals.

5.3 Staying Ahead of Trends

- Monitor trends in AI-generated art and music using tools like TrendSpottr or BuzzSumo.
- Adapt your creative offerings to align with market demands.

6. Challenges and Ethical Considerations

While AI offers unprecedented opportunities, it also raises challenges:

- **Originality**: Ensure your work maintains a unique identity despite AI assistance.
- **Ownership**: Understand intellectual property laws related to AI-generated content.
- **Ethics**: Avoid using AI tools to replicate or plagiarize existing works.

Conclusion: Building Your Creative Empire

AI has redefined what it means to be a creator. With tools that compose symphonies, paint masterpieces, and craft immersive animations, the possibilities are limitless. By integrating AI into your creative process, you can produce high-quality work at scale, reach global audiences, and build a sustainable creative empire.

However, the heart of your empire will always be your vision and passion. Use AI not as a replacement but as a collaborator—one that amplifies your creativity and allows you to achieve more than ever before. With the strategies and tools outlined in this chapter, you're well on your way to crafting a creative empire that stands the test of time.

Chapter 8: AI Storytelling: Breaking into Movies and Gaming

Introduction: The Role of AI in Storytelling

Storytelling has always been the cornerstone of human creativity, shaping movies, video games, and immersive experiences. As entertainment industries evolve, artificial intelligence (AI) is emerging as a powerful collaborator in crafting compelling narratives, dynamic characters, and intricate worlds. From Hollywood to indie game developers, creators are leveraging AI to streamline workflows, generate innovative ideas, and engage audiences like never before.

This chapter delves into how AI is revolutionizing storytelling in movies and gaming, offering tools and techniques for creating memorable scripts, developing intricate game designs, and breaking into these competitive industries.

1. The Evolution of AI in Entertainment

AI has shifted from being a back-end tool for production to a creative partner in storytelling. Key milestones include:

- AI-generated scripts that rival human writers in complexity.
- Procedural world-building and character creation in gaming.
- Real-time audience feedback integration for adaptive storytelling.

2. Crafting Movie Scripts with AI

2.1 Idea Generation for Movies

AI excels at brainstorming and generating fresh ideas:

- **ChatGPT**: Create unique storylines by prompting the AI with themes, genres, or characters.
    - **Example**: "Generate a plot for a science-fiction thriller about time travel."
- **Plotagon**: Visualizes script ideas as animated sequences.

2.2 Writing the Script

AI tools assist in structuring and developing scripts:

- **Jasper AI**: Provides templates for screenplays, dialogue, and action sequences.
    - **Use Case**: Draft scenes efficiently with suggested pacing and tone.
- **Final Draft with AI Features**: Automates script formatting, suggests edits, and tracks character arcs.
    - **Use Case**: Ensure your script meets industry standards.

2.3 Enhancing Character Development

AI can create multidimensional characters:

- **Character.AI**: Builds detailed character profiles with unique traits and backstories.

    - **Use Case**: Develop realistic and relatable characters for your screenplay.
- **Personality Forge**: Simulates character interactions to refine dialogue.

2.4 Analyzing Script Potential

- **ScriptBook AI**: Predicts a screenplay's success based on narrative structure, character appeal, and market trends.
    - **Use Case**: Test your script's potential before pitching to studios.

3. Game Design with AI

Gaming offers unparalleled storytelling potential, combining narratives with interactive elements. AI enables developers to create immersive experiences faster and more efficiently.

3.1 World-Building and Environment Design

AI tools can generate expansive, detailed game worlds:

- **Promethean AI**: Automates the creation of 3D environments, complete with textures and lighting.
  - **Use Case**: Speed up the production of visually stunning game worlds.
- **World Machine**: Generates procedurally designed landscapes for open-world games.
  - **Use Case**: Create realistic terrains with rivers, mountains, and forests.

3.2 Character Design and NPC Development

AI enhances character creation and non-playable character (NPC) behavior:

- **Artbreeder**: Designs unique character models by combining and tweaking traits.
  - **Use Case**: Develop visually distinct characters for your game.
- **Charisma.ai**: Creates emotionally responsive NPCs with lifelike dialogue and reactions.
  - **Use Case**: Enhance immersion by adding depth to NPC interactions.

3.3 Procedural Storytelling

AI enables dynamic narratives that adapt to player choices:

- **Ink by Inkle**: An open-source storytelling engine for branching narratives.
  - **Use Case**: Develop games where player decisions shape the outcome.
- **AI Dungeon**: Generates interactive, text-based adventures based on player input.
  - **Use Case**: Experiment with adaptive storytelling mechanics.

3.4 Gameplay Balancing and Testing

- **Ludeme AI**: Balances game mechanics by simulating thousands of playthroughs.
  - **Use Case**: Optimize difficulty levels and gameplay flow.
- **Unity ML-Agents**: Trains AI agents to test games for bugs and performance issues.

4. AI-Driven Cinematic and Visual Effects
AI simplifies the creation of cinematic sequences and visual effects for movies and games:

- **Runway**: Automates rotoscoping, background removal, and color grading.
  - **Use Case**: Reduce post-production time for film or cutscene visuals.
- **DeepDream Generator**: Enhances visuals with artistic effects or surreal styles.
  - **Use Case**: Add unique aesthetics to game cinematics or movie sequences.

5. Marketing and Audience Engagement with AI
AI extends beyond creation into marketing and audience connection:

- **Trailer Creation**: Tools like **Pictory** automatically generate trailers by analyzing key scenes.
  - **Use Case**: Create promotional content for your movie or game efficiently.
- **Audience Feedback**: Platforms like **MonkeyLearn** analyze social media and reviews to gauge audience sentiment.
  - **Use Case**: Adjust marketing strategies or story elements based on real-time feedback.

6. Monetizing AI-Generated Content in Movies and Gaming
6.1 Crowdfunding Campaigns

- Use AI-generated concept art or trailers to attract backers on platforms like Kickstarter or Indiegogo.

6.2 Licensing and Distribution

- License your AI-generated assets (e.g., characters, environments) to other creators.
- Use platforms like Steam or Amazon Prime to distribute your game or movie.

6.3 Subscription Models and DLCs

- Develop episodic games or movies with subscription-based content.
- AI tools like Charisma.ai can update NPCs or add new dialogue, keeping audiences engaged over time.

7. Ethical Considerations in AI Storytelling

While AI offers immense potential, ethical challenges must be addressed:

- **Originality**: Avoid over-reliance on AI-generated elements that may lack creativity or originality.
- **Ownership**: Establish clear copyright and intellectual property rights for AI-generated content.
- **Representation**: Ensure diverse and accurate representation in AI-generated characters and narratives.

8. Breaking Into the Industry with AI

8.1 Building a Portfolio

- Use AI tools like **DALL·E** or **AIVA** to create concept art or soundtracks for your projects.
- Develop short films or game demos using platforms like **Unity** or **Unreal Engine**.

8.2 Networking with AI

- Use tools like **Lunchclub** to connect with industry professionals.
- Pitch your projects through AI-powered platforms like **Stage 32** or **FilmFreeway**.

8.3 Staying Updated

- Follow AI-driven storytelling trends using tools like **BuzzSumo** and **Google Trends**.

Conclusion: Redefining Storytelling with AI

AI has unlocked a new era of storytelling, merging creativity with cutting-edge technology to create experiences that captivate audiences like never before. Whether you're a filmmaker, game developer, or aspiring creator, AI tools empower you to bring your vision to life with unprecedented efficiency and innovation.

By combining AI's capabilities with your unique creative voice, you can break into the competitive industries of movies and gaming, crafting stories that resonate, entertain, and inspire. The future of storytelling is here—and with AI as your collaborator, the possibilities are limitless.

Part 3: AI in Business and Entrepreneurship

Chapter 9: Starting an AI-Powered Business

Introduction: The Competitive Edge of AI-Powered Businesses

Artificial Intelligence (AI) is no longer a futuristic concept reserved for tech giants; it's a tool accessible to businesses of all sizes, enabling unparalleled efficiency, scalability, and profitability. By automating operations, improving decision-making, and enhancing customer experiences, AI empowers entrepreneurs to create resilient and scalable businesses that thrive in today's fast-paced market.

In this chapter, we'll explore how to start and grow an AI-powered business, leveraging automation, data-driven insights, and innovative tools to optimize operations and maximize growth. Whether you're launching a startup or integrating AI into an existing business, the strategies outlined here will position you for success in the AI-driven economy.

1. The Foundations of an AI-Powered Business

1.1 What is an AI-Powered Business?

An AI-powered business leverages artificial intelligence technologies to automate processes, enhance productivity, and create value. Key characteristics include:

- **Automation**: Replacing manual tasks with AI-driven systems to save time and reduce costs.
- **Data Utilization**: Using AI to analyze large datasets for actionable insights.
- **Customer-Centricity**: Enhancing user experiences through personalization and predictive analytics.

1.2 Benefits of AI in Business

- **Cost Efficiency**: Reduce labor and operational costs through automation.
- **Scalability**: Grow your business without proportional increases in resources.
- **Competitive Advantage**: Stay ahead of competitors by adopting cutting-edge technology.

2. Identifying AI-Powered Business Opportunities

2.1 Choosing the Right Industry

AI can be applied to almost any industry, but some sectors are particularly ripe for innovation:

- **E-Commerce**: AI-driven personalization, inventory management, and customer support.
- **Healthcare**: Predictive analytics, telemedicine, and patient care automation.
- **Finance**: Fraud detection, risk assessment, and robo-advisory services.
- **Creative Industries**: AI-generated content, design, and media production.

2.2 Solving Problems with AI

Start by identifying pain points in your chosen industry:

- **Customer Challenges**: What issues do customers face that AI can solve?
- **Operational Inefficiencies**: Which repetitive tasks can be automated?

- **Market Gaps**: Are there underserved areas where AI can provide value?

2.3 Researching AI Trends

Use tools like **Google Trends**, **CB Insights**, and **Crunchbase** to identify emerging AI applications and investment patterns.

3. Automating Business Operations with AI

3.1 Workflow Automation

- **Zapier**: Connects apps and automates workflows, reducing repetitive tasks.
    - **Use Case**: Automate customer onboarding, invoicing, or email follow-ups.
- **UiPath**: A robotic process automation (RPA) tool that handles complex workflows.
    - **Use Case**: Automate back-office operations like data entry and reporting.

3.2 Customer Service Automation

- **ChatGPT for Customer Support**: AI chatbots that handle customer inquiries 24/7.
    - **Use Case**: Provide instant responses to FAQs and troubleshoot common issues.
- **Zendesk with AI**: Enhances ticket management and customer support through AI-driven insights.
    - **Use Case**: Prioritize tickets based on urgency and sentiment analysis.

3.3 Inventory and Supply Chain Management

- **Blue Yonder**: Predictive analytics for inventory optimization and demand forecasting.
    - **Use Case**: Avoid overstocking or understocking by accurately predicting demand.
- **Llamasoft**: AI-powered supply chain design and logistics optimization.
    - **Use Case**: Streamline shipping and reduce costs.

4. Scaling Your AI-Powered Business

4.1 Data-Driven Decision Making

AI helps scale businesses by providing actionable insights:

- **Tableau with AI**: Visualizes data to uncover trends and inform strategy.
    - **Use Case**: Identify profitable products or markets to focus on.
- **Google Analytics**: Tracks customer behavior and website performance.
    - **Use Case**: Optimize your digital presence to attract more customers.

4.2 Marketing Automation

- **HubSpot AI**: Automates email marketing, lead scoring, and campaign analysis.
    - **Use Case**: Reach your target audience more effectively.
- **AdRoll with AI**: Creates and optimizes ad campaigns across platforms.
    - **Use Case**: Increase ROI on digital advertising.

4.3 Personalization at Scale

- **Dynamic Yield**: Delivers personalized recommendations and experiences to customers.
    - **Use Case**: Enhance customer satisfaction and drive repeat purchases.

5. AI-Powered Tools for Entrepreneurs

5.1 Financial Management

- **QuickBooks AI**: Automates bookkeeping, invoicing, and tax calculations.
  - **Use Case**: Simplify financial management and compliance.
- **Fyle**: AI-driven expense tracking for small businesses.
  - **Use Case**: Monitor spending and identify cost-saving opportunities.

5.2 Project Management

- **Notion AI**: Combines task management with AI-powered brainstorming and documentation.
  - **Use Case**: Streamline team collaboration and project tracking.
- **Asana with AI**: Automates task prioritization and workflow optimization.
  - **Use Case**: Keep projects on schedule and improve productivity.

5.3 Sales Enablement

- **Salesforce Einstein**: AI-enhanced CRM for lead scoring, sales forecasting, and customer insights.
  - **Use Case**: Boost sales efficiency and close deals faster.
- **Pipedrive with AI**: Recommends actions to improve sales performance.
  - **Use Case**: Track and manage your sales pipeline effectively.

6. Monetizing AI-Powered Solutions

6.1 Offering AI as a Service (AIaaS)

- **Custom Solutions**: Build AI-powered tools or platforms tailored to client needs.
  - **Example**: Develop a chatbot service for small businesses.
- **Subscription Models**: Charge recurring fees for access to your AI tools.

6.2 Selling AI-Driven Products

- Create physical or digital products enhanced by AI:
  - **Example**: AI-designed fashion, personalized books, or smart home devices.

6.3 Licensing AI Technology

- Develop proprietary AI models or software and license them to other businesses.

7. Overcoming Challenges in AI-Powered Businesses

7.1 Cost of Implementation

- Start with scalable, cost-effective tools and upgrade as your business grows.
- Leverage cloud-based AI platforms like AWS AI or Google Cloud AI for flexibility.

7.2 Data Privacy and Compliance

- Use tools like **OneTrust** to ensure compliance with GDPR, CCPA, and other regulations.
- Prioritize transparency in how customer data is collected and used.

7.3 Staying Competitive

- Regularly assess industry trends using AI analytics tools.
- Invest in continuous learning and upskilling for yourself and your team.

8. Case Studies: Successful AI-Powered Businesses

8.1 Stitch Fix

- Uses AI to personalize clothing recommendations for customers, driving customer loyalty and reducing returns.

8.2 Grammarly

- A SaaS company that leverages AI to provide writing assistance, generating consistent subscription revenue.

8.3 Lemonade

- An insurance company using AI to process claims quickly and efficiently, reducing overhead and improving customer satisfaction.

Conclusion: Building the Future with AI

Starting an AI-powered business is not just about adopting new technology—it's about embracing a mindset of innovation, efficiency, and scalability. With AI, even small businesses can compete on a global scale, automating routine tasks, delivering exceptional customer experiences, and driving sustainable growth.

By leveraging the strategies and tools outlined in this chapter, you can create a business that thrives in the AI era, positioning yourself not just as an entrepreneur but as a leader in the future of commerce.

Chapter 10: AI Marketing Mastery

Introduction: The New Frontier of Marketing with AI

Marketing has always been a blend of creativity and strategy, but the rise of artificial intelligence (AI) has added a powerful third dimension: data-driven precision. AI enables businesses to craft highly targeted, efficient, and impactful campaigns that resonate deeply with their audiences. From personalized messaging to predictive analytics, AI tools empower marketers to understand consumer behavior, optimize spending, and achieve unparalleled results.

In this chapter, we'll explore how to master AI-driven marketing by leveraging advanced tools, creating data-driven campaigns, and ensuring maximum return on investment (ROI). Whether you're a solopreneur or part of a large organization, these strategies will help you harness AI to transform your marketing efforts.

1. Understanding AI Marketing

1.1 What is AI Marketing?

AI marketing uses artificial intelligence technologies to analyze data, automate tasks, and make decisions that enhance marketing performance. Key components include:

- **Data Analysis**: AI processes vast amounts of data to uncover trends and insights.
- **Automation**: Streamlining repetitive tasks like email marketing and ad targeting.
- **Personalization**: Delivering tailored content to individual consumers.

1.2 Benefits of AI Marketing

- **Improved Targeting**: AI identifies the right audience for your campaigns.
- **Enhanced Creativity**: AI tools generate ideas, content, and visuals.
- **Cost Efficiency**: Automating tasks reduces resource requirements.
- **Real-Time Insights**: Adjust campaigns instantly based on live data.

2. Setting the Foundation for AI Marketing Success

2.1 Establishing Clear Goals

Define measurable objectives for your campaigns, such as:

- Increasing website traffic.
- Generating leads.
- Boosting sales or conversions.

2.2 Building a Strong Data Infrastructure

AI thrives on quality data. Ensure you have systems in place to collect, store, and manage data effectively:

- **Customer Relationship Management (CRM)**: Use tools like **Salesforce** or **HubSpot** to centralize customer data.

- **Data Analytics Platforms**: Implement tools like **Google Analytics** or **Tableau** for real-time data analysis.

2.3 Choosing the Right AI Tools

Identify tools tailored to your needs, whether it's content creation, ad optimization, or audience segmentation.

3. Personalizing Campaigns with AI

3.1 Understanding Your Audience

AI helps you analyze consumer behavior and preferences:

- **Behavioral Analytics**: Tools like **Mixpanel** track user actions on websites and apps.
- **Audience Insights**: Platforms like **Facebook Audience Insights** and **Google Ads Audience Manager** provide demographic and interest data.

3.2 Dynamic Content Personalization

- **Dynamic Yield**: AI-driven personalization engine that tailors website content to individual users.
    - **Use Case**: Display different homepage content based on visitor profiles.
- **Optimove**: Uses predictive analytics to create personalized customer journeys.
    - **Use Case**: Send tailored email campaigns based on purchase history.

4. Creating AI-Enhanced Content

4.1 AI-Powered Content Creation

AI can generate text, visuals, and videos for your campaigns:

- **Jasper AI**: Creates ad copy, blog posts, and social media content.
    - **Use Case**: Write engaging Facebook ads or product descriptions.
- **Canva AI**: Generates custom graphics and design elements.
    - **Use Case**: Design visually stunning Instagram posts or banners.
- **Pictory**: Converts scripts or blog posts into video content with visuals and voiceovers.
    - **Use Case**: Repurpose long-form content into short, shareable videos.

4.2 Optimizing Headlines and Messaging

- **Headline Analyzer by CoSchedule**: Uses AI to score the effectiveness of headlines.
    - **Use Case**: Craft compelling headlines for blog posts and ads.

5. Automating Marketing Campaigns
5.1 Email Marketing Automation

- **Mailchimp with AI**: Automates email campaigns with predictive analytics and personalized recommendations.
    - **Use Case**: Schedule emails to reach audiences at the most effective times.
- **ActiveCampaign**: AI-driven platform for customer segmentation and automated email journeys.
    - **Use Case**: Send tailored product recommendations based on user behavior.

5.2 Social Media Automation

- **Buffer with AI**: Automates post scheduling and suggests optimal posting times.
    - **Use Case**: Maintain consistent social media presence without manual effort.
- **Hootsuite Insights**: Tracks trends and audience engagement for smarter social media strategies.
    - **Use Case**: Identify the best-performing content formats and replicate success.

6. Optimizing Advertising with AI
6.1 AI for Paid Advertising

- **Google Ads with AI**: Automates bidding strategies and identifies the best-performing keywords.
    - **Use Case**: Maximize ROI on search and display ads.
- **AdRoll**: Uses AI to retarget customers with personalized ads across multiple platforms.
    - **Use Case**: Re-engage users who abandoned carts on your website.

6.2 Social Media Advertising

- **Facebook Ads Manager with AI**: Suggests audience segments and optimizes ad placements.
    - **Use Case**: Target niche demographics with precision.
- **TikTok for Business**: Uses AI to identify trending content and tailor ad strategies.
    - **Use Case**: Create ads that align with viral trends for maximum reach.

7. Measuring Campaign Performance with AI
7.1 Real-Time Analytics

- **Google Analytics 4**: Tracks user behavior across platforms and provides actionable insights.
  - **Use Case**: Identify which channels drive the most conversions.
- **Tableau with AI**: Visualizes complex data to uncover trends and patterns.
  - **Use Case**: Monitor campaign performance and refine strategies.

7.2 Predictive Analytics

- **IBM Watson Analytics**: Forecasts campaign outcomes based on historical data.
  - **Use Case**: Adjust budget allocation for future campaigns based on predictive insights.

7.3 A/B Testing with AI

- **Optimizely**: Automates A/B tests for landing pages, ads, and email campaigns.
  - **Use Case**: Determine which variations perform best and scale accordingly.

8. Integrating AI into Your Marketing Team
8.1 Training and Upskilling
Equip your team with the skills needed to leverage AI tools:

- **Online Courses**: Platforms like Coursera and Udemy offer AI marketing courses.
- **Workshops**: Host in-house training sessions to familiarize teams with specific tools.

8.2 Combining Human Creativity with AI
AI enhances creativity but doesn't replace it:

- **Example**: Use AI for data analysis and insights, but rely on human ingenuity for campaign storytelling and emotional connection.

9. Ethical Considerations in AI Marketing

9.1 Transparency

Clearly communicate how data is collected and used.

- **Example**: Include privacy policies and opt-out options for data collection.

9.2 Avoiding Bias

Ensure AI algorithms are unbiased and inclusive:

- Regularly audit AI systems to identify and correct potential biases.

9.3 Respecting Consumer Privacy

Comply with regulations like GDPR and CCPA to protect user data.

Conclusion: Mastering AI Marketing for Maximum Impact

AI marketing is more than a trend—it's a transformative approach that empowers businesses to connect with audiences on a deeper, more personalized level. By integrating AI into your marketing strategy, you can optimize performance, reduce costs, and achieve unprecedented results.

The key to success lies in balancing AI's capabilities with human creativity and ethical practices. By applying the tools and strategies outlined in this chapter, you can master AI-driven marketing and create campaigns that resonate, engage, and convert, propelling your brand to new heights in the digital landscape.

Chapter 11: E-commerce Domination with AI

Introduction: AI as the Ultimate E-commerce Game-Changer

E-commerce has revolutionized the way people shop, and artificial intelligence (AI) is further reshaping the industry by enhancing user experiences, streamlining operations, and driving unprecedented growth. AI-driven technologies empower businesses to create personalized shopping experiences, recommend products with precision, and anticipate customer needs like never before. These capabilities are not just for retail giants like Amazon or Alibaba—AI tools are increasingly accessible to businesses of all sizes.

This chapter explores how to leverage AI for e-commerce domination by building product recommendation engines, optimizing user experiences, and creating strategies to stay ahead of the competition.

1. The Role of AI in E-commerce

1.1 What is AI in E-commerce?

AI in e-commerce refers to the application of artificial intelligence technologies to automate tasks, analyze customer behavior, and optimize shopping experiences.

- **Key Components**:
  - Personalized product recommendations.
  - Dynamic pricing models.
  - Inventory and supply chain optimization.
  - Predictive analytics for customer behavior.

1.2 Benefits of AI in E-commerce

- **Personalization**: Tailored experiences that increase customer satisfaction and loyalty.
- **Efficiency**: Automated processes that save time and reduce costs.
- **Growth**: Data-driven insights that unlock new revenue streams and market opportunities.

2. Building AI-Driven Product Recommendation Systems

2.1 How Recommendation Engines Work

AI-powered recommendation systems analyze customer data to suggest relevant products. These systems typically use:

- **Collaborative Filtering**: Identifies similarities between users based on their interactions.
- **Content-Based Filtering**: Recommends products similar to those a user has viewed or purchased.
- **Hybrid Systems**: Combines collaborative and content-based filtering for greater accuracy.

2.2 Tools for Building Recommendation Engines

- **Google Cloud Recommendations AI**: Provides scalable, real-time personalized product recommendations.
  - **Use Case**: Implement on your e-commerce platform to boost sales.
- **AWS Personalize**: Offers customizable recommendation models powered by machine learning.
  - **Use Case**: Create targeted product suggestions for repeat customers.
- **Algolia Recommend**: Delivers AI-driven recommendations directly within search results.
  - **Use Case**: Enhance on-site search functionality with personalized product recommendations.

2.3 Optimizing Recommendations

- Use A/B testing to evaluate the effectiveness of different recommendation algorithms.
- Incorporate real-time data such as browsing history and cart activity to refine suggestions.
- Personalize recommendations based on customer segments (e.g., new vs. returning customers).

3. Enhancing User Experience (UX) with AI

3.1 Personalized Shopping Experiences

AI enables businesses to create individualized experiences for every shopper:

- **Dynamic Website Content**: Platforms like **Dynamic Yield** adjust homepage banners, product displays, and promotions based on user behavior.
    - **Use Case**: Display "Recommended for You" sections tailored to individual preferences.
- **Chatbots and Virtual Assistants**: Tools like **ChatGPT** or **Zendesk AI** provide instant, 24/7 customer support.
    - **Use Case**: Assist users with product searches, FAQs, and order tracking.

3.2 Visual and Voice Search

AI-powered visual and voice search features simplify the shopping experience:

- **Visual Search**: Platforms like **Syte** allow customers to upload images and find similar products.
    - **Use Case**: Attract visually-driven shoppers by enabling product discovery through photos.
- **Voice Search**: Integrate AI tools like **Google Dialogflow** or **Alexa Skills Kit** to enable voice-activated shopping.
    - **Use Case**: Capture customers using smart speakers for hands-free shopping.

3.3 Augmented Reality (AR) Integration

AI-enhanced AR tools create immersive shopping experiences:

- **IKEA Place**: Lets customers visualize furniture in their homes using AI-driven AR.
    - **Use Case**: Reduce returns by giving customers confidence in their purchases.
- **Zara's AR App**: Offers virtual fitting rooms to try on clothes digitally.

4. AI for E-commerce Operations

4.1 Inventory Management

AI predicts demand trends to optimize inventory levels:

- **Blue Yonder Luminate**: An AI-powered supply chain tool for demand forecasting.
    - **Use Case**: Avoid overstocking or running out of high-demand items.
- **IBM Sterling Supply Chain**: Tracks inventory in real-time and automates reordering processes.

4.2 Logistics and Shipping

AI streamlines shipping and delivery:

- **Route Optimization**: Tools like **Onfleet AI** calculate the fastest, most cost-effective delivery routes.
    - **Use Case**: Improve delivery times and reduce shipping costs.
- **Predictive Logistics**: Use AI to predict delays and provide accurate delivery estimates.

4.3 Fraud Detection

AI identifies fraudulent transactions by analyzing patterns in real-time:

- **Sift**: Detects and prevents fraud in payment processing.
    - **Use Case**: Protect your business and customers from fraudulent activities.
- **Forter**: Automates fraud detection while maintaining a seamless checkout experience.

5. AI-Driven Marketing for E-commerce

5.1 Predictive Analytics for Customer Behavior

- **Tools like Pega AI** analyze past purchase behavior to forecast future actions.
    - **Use Case:** Target high-value customers with tailored promotions.

5.2 Dynamic Pricing

AI adjusts prices based on market demand, competitor pricing, and inventory levels:

- **Prisync**: Monitors competitor prices and automates pricing strategies.
    - **Use Case:** Stay competitive without sacrificing profitability.

5.3 Automated Email Campaigns

- **Klaviyo with AI**: Creates personalized email sequences based on user behavior.
    - **Use Case:** Send abandoned cart reminders or post-purchase follow-ups.

5.4 Social Media and Advertising

- **AdRoll with AI**: Retargets website visitors with personalized ads across platforms.
    - **Use Case:** Convert window shoppers into buyers.
- **TikTok for Business**: Uses AI to identify trends and optimize ad placement.

6. Measuring Performance and Optimizing with AI

6.1 Conversion Rate Optimization (CRO)

- **Hotjar AI**: Analyzes user interactions to identify pain points in the shopping journey.
    - **Use Case:** Optimize your website's layout and checkout process.
- **Crazy Egg**: Provides heatmaps and session recordings to understand user behavior.

6.2 Customer Feedback Analysis

- **MonkeyLearn**: Uses AI to analyze customer reviews and social media sentiment.
    - **Use Case:** Identify areas for improvement in product offerings or service quality.

6.3 Sales Forecasting

- **Tableau with AI**: Visualizes sales trends and predicts future performance.
    - **Use Case:** Make informed decisions about inventory and marketing spend.

7. Scaling Your E-commerce Business with AI

7.1 Expanding Globally

AI simplifies the complexities of international e-commerce:

- **Language Translation**: Tools like **Weglot** or **Google Translate AI** make websites multilingual.
  - **Use Case**: Reach global audiences with localized content.
- **Currency Conversion**: AI-enabled platforms automatically adjust prices based on location.

7.2 Subscription Models

AI helps optimize subscription-based businesses:

- **Chargebee with AI**: Automates billing and renewals for subscription services.
  - **Use Case**: Increase retention rates with personalized offers for subscribers.

7.3 Customer Retention

- **Loyalty Programs**: Platforms like **Smile.io** use AI to analyze customer spending and incentivize repeat purchases.

8. Challenges and Ethical Considerations

8.1 Data Privacy

Ensure compliance with data protection laws like GDPR and CCPA.

- Use tools like **OneTrust** to manage user consent and data collection.

8.2 Avoiding Algorithm Bias

Regularly audit AI systems to ensure fairness in recommendations and pricing.

8.3 Balancing Automation and Human Touch

While AI enhances efficiency, maintaining human oversight ensures personalized and empathetic customer service.

Conclusion: Dominating E-commerce with AI

AI is not just a tool but a transformative force in e-commerce. By integrating AI-driven recommendation systems, enhancing user experiences, and optimizing operations, businesses can dominate their markets and scale effectively. The strategies outlined in this chapter provide a roadmap for leveraging AI to its fullest potential, empowering you to create an e-commerce powerhouse that thrives in the digital age.

With the right tools, data-driven insights, and innovative approaches, you can position your e-commerce business as a leader in the AI-powered future of retail.

Chapter 12: Passive Income Streams with AI

Introduction: Unlocking Passive Income in the Age of AI

Passive income, the dream of earning money with minimal ongoing effort, has been transformed by artificial intelligence (AI). AI tools and strategies enable individuals and businesses to set up and maintain income-generating systems with unparalleled efficiency and scalability. Whether through dropshipping, digital products, or memberships, AI helps automate operations, enhance customer experiences, and optimize revenue streams.

In this chapter, we'll explore how to harness AI to create, manage, and scale passive income streams. You'll learn actionable strategies and tools to build a sustainable income source while freeing up your time for other pursuits.

1. What is Passive Income in the AI Era?

Passive income refers to revenue streams that require minimal ongoing effort to maintain. AI enhances passive income generation by:

- Automating processes like marketing, customer service, and inventory management.
- Analyzing data to optimize revenue strategies.
- Scaling operations with minimal additional resources.

Common AI-powered passive income streams include:

- Dropshipping.
- Digital products (eBooks, courses, software).
- Membership sites and subscription models.

2. Dropshipping with AI

Dropshipping, where products are sold without holding inventory, is one of the most accessible passive income streams. AI simplifies and enhances this business model.

2.1 Setting Up a Dropshipping Business

- **Shopify with AI**: Use AI-powered Shopify apps like **Oberlo** to source products, manage orders, and automate fulfillment.
    - **Use Case**: Import products from suppliers and list them on your store with a single click.
- **Spocket**: An AI-driven platform that connects you with suppliers offering high-quality products.
    - **Use Case**: Focus on fast shipping by selecting suppliers based in your target region.

2.2 Optimizing Product Selection with AI

- **Sell The Trend**: An AI tool that identifies trending products based on market data.
    - **Use Case**: Choose high-demand products to maximize sales potential.

- **Zik Analytics**: Helps analyze eBay and Amazon trends to identify profitable products.

2.3 Automating Marketing and Customer Support

- **AdRoll**: Uses AI to automate retargeting ads for visitors who didn't complete purchases.
  - **Use Case**: Increase conversion rates with personalized ads.
- **Tidio AI Chatbot**: Provides 24/7 customer support to answer FAQs and assist with orders.
  - **Use Case**: Improve customer satisfaction and reduce cart abandonment rates.

3. Digital Products with AI

Digital products are infinitely scalable and require no inventory. AI tools make it easier to create, market, and manage these products.

3.1 Creating Digital Products with AI

- **eBooks and Courses**:
    - Use **ChatGPT** to write eBooks or create course scripts.
        - **Example**: Prompt ChatGPT with "Create a 10-module outline for an online course on personal finance."
    - Use **Canva AI** to design eBook layouts and course visuals.
        - **Use Case**: Develop visually appealing products without hiring a designer.
- **Software and Apps**:
    - Use AI platforms like **Bubble** or **Adalo** to create no-code applications.
        - **Use Case**: Develop tools like budgeting apps or productivity trackers without programming skills.

3.2 Selling Digital Products

- **Gumroad**: AI-optimized platform for selling digital downloads and memberships.
    - **Use Case**: Monetize eBooks, courses, or templates directly to your audience.
- **Teachable with AI**: Offers course-building tools with analytics to track learner progress.
    - **Use Case**: Host and sell your online courses with minimal effort.

3.3 Marketing Digital Products with AI

- **Jarvis AI (Jasper)**: Creates sales copy and ad campaigns tailored to your audience.
    - **Use Case**: Write compelling product descriptions and email marketing sequences.
- **Optimizely**: Uses AI for A/B testing sales pages and optimizing conversion rates.

4. Membership Sites and Subscription Models

Membership and subscription models provide consistent, recurring income. AI tools enhance member engagement and automate management.

4.1 Creating a Membership Platform

- **MemberPress**: An AI-enhanced platform for building and managing membership sites.
    - **Use Case**: Offer exclusive content, resources, or community access for a monthly fee.
- **Podia**: Combines membership management with course hosting and digital downloads.
    - **Use Case**: Monetize multiple income streams from one platform.

4.2 Personalizing Member Experiences

- **Dynamic Yield**: Uses AI to customize content for individual members.
    - **Use Case**: Display personalized course recommendations based on user activity.
- **Intercom with AI**: Enhances customer interactions by providing tailored support and recommendations.

4.3 Engaging Members with AI

- **HubSpot CRM with AI**: Tracks member engagement and automates communication.
    - **Use Case**: Send renewal reminders and personalized messages to inactive members.
- **ManyChat**: AI-powered chatbots for membership communities.
    - **Use Case**: Facilitate real-time interactions and updates in your community.

5. Marketing and Scaling Passive Income Streams with AI
5.1 Search Engine Optimization (SEO)

- **Surfer SEO**: An AI tool that optimizes content for search engines.
  - **Use Case**: Increase organic traffic to your digital products or memberships.
- **Ahrefs with AI**: Provides keyword research and backlink analysis.
  - **Use Case**: Identify high-performing keywords and boost your site's visibility.

5.2 Social Media Automation

- **Hootsuite Insights**: Uses AI to track trends and optimize social media campaigns.
  - **Use Case**: Post regularly and engage with your audience without manual effort.
- **Lately AI**: Repurposes long-form content into social media posts.
  - **Use Case**: Save time creating posts while maintaining consistent branding.

5.3 Data-Driven Scaling

- **Tableau with AI**: Visualizes sales data to identify growth opportunities.
  - **Use Case**: Analyze which products or services generate the most revenue.
- **Google Analytics 4**: Tracks user behavior and conversion rates.
  - **Use Case**: Optimize sales funnels for better performance.

6. Managing Passive Income Streams with AI
6.1 Automating Financial Processes

- **QuickBooks AI**: Automates bookkeeping, invoicing, and expense tracking.
  - **Use Case**: Keep your financial records organized without manual effort.
- **Fyle**: Tracks expenses and automates reporting.

6.2 Handling Customer Support

- **Freshdesk with AI**: Provides AI-powered ticketing and support systems.
  - **Use Case**: Address customer inquiries efficiently, even at scale.
- **Drift AI Chatbot**: Engages customers with conversational AI for support and upselling.

7. Ethical Considerations in AI-Powered Passive Income

7.1 Transparency

Clearly disclose the use of AI in your business, especially for customer interactions.

7.2 Data Privacy

Ensure compliance with GDPR, CCPA, and other data protection regulations. Use tools like **OneTrust** to manage user consent.

7.3 Balancing Automation and Personalization

While AI automates many tasks, ensure a human touch in areas like customer support and community engagement.

Conclusion: Achieving Financial Freedom with AI

AI has made creating and managing passive income streams more accessible than ever. By leveraging the tools and strategies outlined in this chapter, you can establish automated systems that generate consistent revenue while freeing up your time.

Whether you're running a dropshipping store, selling digital products, or managing a membership platform, AI can optimize every aspect of your business. The key to success lies in continuously analyzing data, refining your approach, and embracing innovation. With AI as your partner, financial freedom is no longer a distant dream but an achievable reality.

Part 4: AI in Investment Strategies

Chapter 13: AI in Stock Market Analysis

Introduction: Revolutionizing Stock Market Analysis with AI

The stock market has long been considered one of the most complex and volatile financial systems. Success requires a deep understanding of market trends, extensive research, and the ability to make informed decisions quickly. With the advent of artificial intelligence (AI), stock market analysis has undergone a paradigm shift. AI-powered tools can process vast amounts of data in real-time, uncover patterns, and provide predictive insights that were previously impossible to achieve.

This chapter explores how AI is revolutionizing stock market analysis by enabling predictive modeling, automating trading strategies, and enhancing decision-making for both individual investors and institutional traders.

1. The Role of AI in Stock Market Analysis

1.1 Why AI is Perfect for Stock Market Analysis

- **Data Processing at Scale**: AI analyzes financial reports, news, and historical market data faster than human analysts.
- **Pattern Recognition**: AI algorithms detect subtle patterns in price movements and trading volumes.
- **Predictive Capabilities**: AI uses machine learning to forecast stock prices and market trends.

1.2 Benefits of AI in the Stock Market

- **Speed and Efficiency**: AI processes data in real-time, enabling faster decision-making.
- **Reduced Emotional Bias**: Algorithms eliminate the emotional factors that can cloud human judgment.
- **Accessibility**: AI democratizes access to sophisticated trading tools for retail investors.

2. Key AI Techniques Used in Stock Market Analysis

2.1 Machine Learning (ML)

- **Supervised Learning**: Algorithms trained on historical data predict future trends.
- **Unsupervised Learning**: Identifies anomalies or clusters of behavior in trading patterns.
- **Reinforcement Learning**: AI systems improve trading strategies through trial and error.

2.2 Natural Language Processing (NLP)

- Analyzes financial news, earnings calls, and social media sentiment to gauge market mood.
    - **Example**: AI detects a surge in positive sentiment around a company and predicts a stock price increase.

2.3 Predictive Analytics

- Combines historical data and real-time inputs to forecast stock prices and market movements.

2.4 Algorithmic Trading

- Uses AI to automate trading strategies, optimizing entry and exit points for trades.

3. Tools and Platforms for AI-Driven Stock Market Analysis

3.1 Retail Investor Tools

- **Trade Ideas**: AI-powered platform for identifying trading opportunities based on real-time data.
    - **Use Case**: Receive alerts for high-potential trades in volatile markets.
- **Tickeron**: Provides AI-driven predictions for stock movements and trend analysis.
    - **Use Case**: Access buy/sell signals with confidence scores for informed decisions.
- **Zerodha Streak**: Enables retail investors to create, backtest, and automate trading strategies using AI.

3.2 Institutional Tools

- **Kavout**: Offers predictive stock rankings based on AI-driven insights.
    - **Use Case**: Institutions use Kavout to optimize portfolios and asset allocations.
- **Sentifi**: Monitors market sentiment across social media, news, and blogs to provide actionable insights.
    - **Use Case**: Detect early market trends or anomalies before they become mainstream.

3.3 Data Aggregation Platforms

- **Quandl**: Provides access to alternative data sets for quantitative analysis.
    - **Use Case**: Enhance trading models with non-traditional data like weather or economic indicators.
- **Yahoo Finance API**: Integrates real-time stock data into custom AI models.

4. Predictive Analysis in Stock Market Decisions
4.1 Analyzing Historical Data

- AI identifies long-term trends by analyzing historical stock prices, volume, and technical indicators.
- Tools like **MetaTrader 5** and **QuantConnect** allow backtesting of AI-driven models.

4.2 Real-Time Data Processing

- AI platforms like **Alpaca** provide real-time data feeds for instant analysis.
- **Use Case**: Detect sudden price changes and capitalize on short-term opportunities.

4.3 Sentiment Analysis for Market Predictions

- **SentiStock**: Uses NLP to analyze investor sentiment from financial news and social media.
    - **Use Case**: Anticipate market shifts driven by public opinion or breaking news.

4.4 Risk Assessment and Portfolio Optimization

- AI calculates risk metrics like Sharpe ratios and volatility.
- **BlackRock's Aladdin Platform**: Combines AI and risk analytics to optimize institutional portfolios.

5. Algorithmic and High-Frequency Trading with AI

5.1 How Algorithmic Trading Works

- Uses AI algorithms to execute trades automatically based on pre-defined criteria.
- Benefits:
    - Faster execution speeds.
    - Reduced transaction costs.
    - Minimized human error.

5.2 High-Frequency Trading (HFT)

- AI analyzes market microstructure to make trades within milliseconds.
    - **Example**: AI detects an arbitrage opportunity between two markets and executes trades instantly.

5.3 Platforms for Algorithmic Trading

- **Interactive Brokers API**: Enables algorithmic trading for advanced users.
- **Quantopian**: Provides a collaborative platform for developing and testing trading algorithms.

6. AI-Driven Risk Management

6.1 Identifying Market Risks

- AI detects anomalies in trading behavior or market conditions.
    - **Example**: A sudden spike in volatility alerts investors to potential risks.

6.2 Diversifying Portfolios with AI

- AI recommends optimal asset allocations based on risk tolerance and market conditions.
- **Betterment**: A robo-advisor that uses AI to create personalized investment portfolios.

6.3 Fraud Detection

- AI monitors trading activity to identify potential fraud or market manipulation.

7. Ethical and Practical Considerations
7.1 Avoiding Over-Reliance on AI

- While AI enhances decision-making, it's crucial to maintain human oversight.

7.2 Addressing Data Bias

- Regularly audit AI models to ensure fair and unbiased predictions.

7.3 Regulatory Compliance

- Stay informed about regulations surrounding AI-driven trading, such as those set by the SEC or FINRA.

8. Strategies for Individual Investors Using AI
8.1 Leveraging AI for Stock Screening

- Use platforms like **Finviz** or **Stock Rover** to filter stocks based on AI-driven insights.

8.2 Incorporating AI Tools into Investment Strategy

- Combine AI predictions with fundamental analysis for a holistic approach.

8.3 Monitoring and Adjusting

- Use AI analytics tools like **Portfolio Visualizer** to track performance and make adjustments.

9. Future Trends in AI and Stock Market Analysis

- **AI-Driven ESG Investing**: Identifying sustainable and ethical investment opportunities using AI.
- **Quantum Computing in Trading**: Enhancing AI algorithms with quantum computing for faster analysis.
- **Real-Time Global Market Analysis**: AI integrating multiple international data sources for holistic market insights.

Conclusion: Empowering Investors with AI

AI is revolutionizing stock market analysis by making it more accessible, efficient, and precise. By integrating AI tools and techniques into your investment strategy, you can gain a competitive edge, reduce risks, and make informed decisions based on real-time insights.

The key to mastering AI in stock market analysis lies in balancing technology with human intuition and maintaining a disciplined approach. With the strategies outlined in this chapter, you're equipped to leverage AI to navigate the complexities of the stock market and achieve your financial goals.

Chapter 14: Cryptocurrency Wealth with AI

Introduction: The Intersection of AI and Cryptocurrency

Cryptocurrency markets are known for their volatility, operating 24/7 and often experiencing rapid price fluctuations. While this dynamic environment offers immense opportunities for wealth creation, it also presents significant risks. Artificial intelligence (AI) has emerged as a powerful tool to navigate these complexities, providing traders with real-time insights, predictive analytics, and automated trading strategies to optimize their performance.

In this chapter, we'll explore how AI algorithms are revolutionizing cryptocurrency trading, from identifying profitable opportunities to managing risk effectively. Whether you're a novice or an experienced trader, AI can help you make informed decisions and capitalize on the growing crypto market.

1. The Role of AI in Cryptocurrency Trading

1.1 Why AI is a Game-Changer for Crypto Trading

- **Real-Time Data Processing**: AI can analyze vast amounts of data, including market trends, news, and social media sentiment, in real time.
- **Predictive Modeling**: Machine learning models forecast price movements with high accuracy by identifying historical patterns.
- **Automation**: AI-powered bots execute trades instantly, ensuring you don't miss opportunities in a fast-moving market.

1.2 Benefits of AI in Cryptocurrency Trading

- **Improved Decision-Making**: Data-driven insights reduce emotional trading decisions.
- **Scalability**: AI enables traders to monitor multiple cryptocurrencies and exchanges simultaneously.
- **Risk Mitigation**: Algorithms optimize stop-loss levels and manage portfolio risk effectively.

2. Key AI Techniques in Crypto Trading

2.1 Machine Learning

- **Supervised Learning**: Models trained on historical data predict future price movements.
- **Unsupervised Learning**: Identifies hidden patterns in market behavior, such as clustering price movements.
- **Reinforcement Learning**: AI learns optimal trading strategies by simulating trades in various market conditions.

2.2 Natural Language Processing (NLP)

- Analyzes news, social media, and forums like Twitter and Reddit to gauge market sentiment.
    - **Example**: Detecting a surge in positive sentiment for Bitcoin could indicate a potential price rise.

2.3 Sentiment Analysis

- AI tools measure public perception of specific cryptocurrencies to anticipate market movements.
    - **Example**: Using sentiment analysis on tweets to identify upcoming market trends.

2.4 Predictive Analytics

- Combines historical data and real-time inputs to forecast future price trends.

3. Tools and Platforms for AI-Driven Crypto Trading

3.1 Trading Bots and Algorithms

- **3Commas**: Offers AI-driven bots for automated trading with customizable strategies.
  - **Use Case**: Set up grid trading bots to capitalize on market volatility.
- **Cryptohopper**: Provides AI-powered signals and automated trading strategies.
  - **Use Case**: Leverage pre-configured trading strategies or create custom ones.
- **Pionex**: Features built-in AI bots for arbitrage, grid trading, and dollar-cost averaging.

3.2 Market Sentiment Tools

- **Santiment**: Tracks market sentiment, on-chain data, and social media trends.
  - **Use Case**: Use sentiment analysis to identify bullish or bearish market conditions.
- **LunarCrush**: Analyzes social media activity to provide actionable insights for crypto traders.
  - **Use Case**: Spot emerging trends before they reflect in price movements.

3.3 Predictive Analytics Platforms

- **QuantConnect**: A quantitative trading platform that supports algorithmic crypto trading.
  - **Use Case**: Develop and backtest machine learning models for crypto trading strategies.
- **Shrimpy**: Offers portfolio management and predictive analytics.
  - **Use Case**: Optimize portfolio performance by reallocating assets based on AI predictions.

4. Creating an AI-Powered Crypto Trading Strategy
4.1 Defining Your Trading Goals

- Identify whether your focus is on short-term gains, long-term investment, or arbitrage opportunities.
- Establish clear risk tolerance and capital allocation strategies.

4.2 Data Collection and Preprocessing

- Use APIs from exchanges like Binance or Coinbase to collect historical and real-time market data.
- Incorporate alternative data sources, such as social media sentiment and blockchain activity.

4.3 Designing Your Algorithm

- **Entry and Exit Points**: Define criteria for buying and selling, such as moving averages or momentum indicators.
- **Risk Management**: Include stop-loss orders, trailing stops, and position sizing rules.
- **Backtesting**: Test your strategy on historical data using platforms like QuantConnect or AlgoTrader.

4.4 Deploying and Monitoring Your AI Bot

- Use cloud-based platforms to run your trading bot continuously.
- Monitor performance metrics and adjust strategies based on real-time results.

5. AI in Portfolio Management

5.1 Diversification with AI

- AI tools analyze correlations between cryptocurrencies to create diversified portfolios.
  - **Example**: Reduce risk by balancing Bitcoin, Ethereum, and stablecoins like USDT.

5.2 Rebalancing Strategies

- Platforms like **Shrimpy** automatically rebalance portfolios based on AI-driven insights.
  - **Use Case**: Maintain target asset allocations in volatile markets.

5.3 Risk Management with AI

- Use AI to calculate Value at Risk (VaR) and optimize portfolio allocations.
- Tools like **AlphaSense** provide risk assessments for individual assets.

6. Advanced AI Techniques in Crypto Trading

6.1 Arbitrage Trading

- AI identifies price discrepancies across exchanges and executes trades to profit from the difference.
  - **Example**: Buying Bitcoin on Kraken and selling it on Binance at a higher price.

6.2 High-Frequency Trading (HFT)

- Leverages AI to execute trades within milliseconds, capitalizing on micro-fluctuations in price.
  - **Platforms**: Use advanced trading systems like QuantConnect for HFT strategies.

6.3 Predicting Market Crashes

- AI detects anomalies in trading volumes, sentiment, or blockchain activity to anticipate downturns.

7. Challenges and Risks of Using AI in Crypto Trading

7.1 Overfitting in Models

- AI models may perform well on historical data but fail in live markets due to overfitting.
- **Solution**: Regularly validate models with out-of-sample data.

7.2 Data Quality

- Inaccurate or incomplete data can lead to poor model performance.
- **Solution**: Use reliable data sources and clean data before analysis.

7.3 Regulatory Uncertainty

- Cryptocurrency regulations vary by country and may impact AI-driven trading.
- **Solution**: Stay informed about compliance requirements in your trading jurisdiction.

7.4 Market Volatility

- AI models must adapt to sudden market shifts that may not align with historical trends.

8. Ethical and Security Considerations

8.1 Ethical AI Use

- Avoid exploiting market inefficiencies in ways that may harm other traders.
- Promote transparency in algorithmic trading practices.

8.2 Security Measures

- Use secure APIs with two-factor authentication for exchange integration.
- Regularly update and monitor trading bots to prevent hacking attempts.

9. Future Trends in AI and Crypto Trading

- **Quantum Computing**: The next leap in processing power may revolutionize crypto trading algorithms.
- **Decentralized AI Platforms**: Blockchain-based AI systems that offer enhanced transparency and security.
- **AI-Powered DAOs**: Decentralized autonomous organizations using AI to manage crypto investments.

Conclusion: Mastering Cryptocurrency Wealth with AI

AI has become a transformative force in cryptocurrency trading, enabling traders to make data-driven decisions, automate strategies, and maximize profits. However, success requires continuous learning, careful risk management, and an understanding of the limitations of AI models.

By implementing the tools, strategies, and best practices outlined in this chapter, you can harness the power of AI to build wealth in the cryptocurrency market while navigating its complexities with confidence. The future of crypto trading belongs to those who embrace innovation, and AI is the ultimate tool for staying ahead of the curve.

Chapter 15: Real Estate Optimization

Introduction: Revolutionizing Real Estate with AI

Real estate is one of the most lucrative and stable investment sectors, but it requires careful analysis, strategic decision-making, and significant time commitments. Artificial intelligence (AI) is reshaping how investors, property managers, and real estate professionals approach the industry. By automating complex tasks such as property valuation, market analysis, and investment predictions, AI allows stakeholders to make smarter, faster, and more profitable decisions.

This chapter explores how AI can optimize real estate investment strategies, assist in property flipping, and streamline portfolio management. Whether you're a seasoned investor or a beginner, AI tools can help you gain a competitive edge in the ever-evolving real estate market.

1. The Role of AI in Real Estate Optimization

1.1 How AI is Changing Real Estate

AI tools analyze vast amounts of data to provide insights into market trends, property values, and investment opportunities. Key benefits include:

- **Accurate Valuation**: AI estimates property values based on real-time data and market conditions.
- **Market Forecasting**: Predicts future trends to inform long-term investment strategies.
- **Streamlined Processes**: Automates tasks such as tenant screening, portfolio management, and marketing.

1.2 Benefits of AI in Real Estate

- **Increased Efficiency**: Reduces manual effort in property research and evaluation.
- **Enhanced Accuracy**: Minimizes errors in valuations and risk assessments.
- **Data-Driven Decisions**: Provides actionable insights for better investment outcomes.

2. AI Tools for Property Valuation

2.1 How AI Determines Property Value

AI algorithms use data from multiple sources, including:

- Historical sales data.
- Comparable property prices.
- Neighborhood trends.
- Amenities and infrastructure development.

2.2 Popular AI Tools for Property Valuation

- **Zillow Zestimate**: Uses AI to estimate property values based on location, square footage, and market trends.
    - **Use Case**: Quickly assess the value of residential properties.
- **Reonomy**: An AI-driven platform for commercial property valuation and market analysis.
    - **Use Case**: Evaluate the profitability of office buildings, retail spaces, and industrial properties.
- **HouseCanary**: Provides real-time property valuations and forecasts.
    - **Use Case**: Use predictive analytics to determine future property values.

2.3 Improving Valuation Accuracy with AI

- **AI-Enhanced Visual Analysis**: Tools like Restb.ai analyze property images to assess condition and quality.
- **Dynamic Data Updates**: Platforms integrate real-time market data to keep valuations current.

3. AI in Real Estate Flipping

Flipping properties—buying, renovating, and reselling them for profit—requires precise timing and resource allocation. AI simplifies this process by providing actionable insights.

3.1 Identifying Profitable Properties

- **Mashvisor**: Analyzes potential rental income and cash flow for residential properties.
  - **Use Case**: Find undervalued properties with high resale potential.
- **PropStream**: Uses AI to identify off-market deals and distressed properties.
  - **Use Case**: Locate homes suitable for flipping before they hit the market.

3.2 Predicting Renovation Costs with AI

- **Hover**: Creates 3D property models to estimate renovation costs and timelines.
  - **Use Case**: Budget accurately for repairs and improvements.
- **Estimator360**: Uses AI to calculate material and labor costs for remodeling projects.

3.3 Optimizing Resale Strategies

- AI tools analyze local market conditions to determine the best time to sell.
- Platforms like **Redfin AI** suggest optimal pricing based on current demand.

4. AI-Driven Real Estate Investment Strategies

4.1 Analyzing Market Trends

- **CoreLogic**: Tracks property market performance and forecasts future trends.
  - **Use Case**: Identify emerging neighborhoods with high growth potential.
- **CoStar**: Provides in-depth data on commercial real estate trends.
  - **Use Case**: Make informed decisions about retail, office, or industrial investments.

4.2 Portfolio Diversification

AI assists in balancing risk by analyzing:

- Geographical diversification.
- Property types (residential, commercial, industrial).
- Economic indicators affecting real estate performance.

4.3 Risk Assessment with AI

- **CrediFi**: Evaluates the financial health of properties and associated risks.
  - **Use Case**: Minimize investment risks in high-stakes markets.
- **BuildFax**: Uses historical property data to assess maintenance risks.

5. AI for Property Management
5.1 Tenant Screening and Onboarding

- **TurboTenant**: Uses AI to screen tenants based on credit scores, rental history, and income.
    - **Use Case**: Reduce the risk of problematic tenants.
- **AppFolio**: Automates lease management and tenant communications.
    - **Use Case**: Streamline property management tasks.

5.2 Maintenance and Repairs

- **Fixflo**: AI-driven tool that predicts maintenance issues and schedules repairs.
    - **Use Case**: Prevent costly damages by addressing issues early.

5.3 Rent Optimization

- **Rentometer**: AI analyzes local rental market trends to suggest optimal pricing.
    - **Use Case**: Maximize rental income without overpricing.

6. Marketing Real Estate with AI
6.1 Virtual Tours and Visualization

- **Matterport**: Creates AI-powered 3D virtual tours of properties.
    - **Use Case**: Attract buyers and renters with immersive property experiences.

6.2 Targeted Advertising

- **Adwerx**: Uses AI to create hyper-local ads for properties.
    - **Use Case**: Reach the right audience with precision-targeted campaigns.
- **Facebook Ads with AI**: Automatically optimizes real estate ads for engagement.

6.3 Lead Generation

- **CINC**: AI identifies and nurtures potential buyers or renters.
    - **Use Case**: Convert leads into clients more effectively.

7. Challenges and Ethical Considerations

7.1 Data Privacy and Security

- Protect tenant and buyer information by complying with regulations like GDPR and CCPA.

7.2 Avoiding Over-Reliance on AI

- Use AI as a tool to complement, not replace, human expertise and intuition.

7.3 Algorithmic Bias

- Regularly audit AI systems to ensure fair and unbiased outcomes in valuations and tenant screening.

8. Future Trends in AI for Real Estate

- **Blockchain Integration**: AI combined with blockchain for secure property transactions.
- **Green Building Analytics**: AI assessing energy efficiency and sustainability of properties.
- **Smart Cities**: AI shaping urban planning and real estate development.

Conclusion: Maximizing Real Estate Potential with AI

AI is transforming the real estate industry by enabling more accurate valuations, smarter investment decisions, and efficient property management. By leveraging the tools and strategies outlined in this chapter, you can optimize your real estate ventures, reduce risks, and maximize returns.

Whether you're flipping properties, building a rental portfolio, or managing commercial assets, AI equips you with the insights and automation needed to thrive in a competitive market. The future of real estate lies in data-driven decisions, and AI is your key to unlocking its full potential.

Chapter 16: Angel Investing with AI

Introduction: Transforming Angel Investing with AI

Angel investing involves providing early-stage funding to startups in exchange for equity. While the potential returns can be significant, the risks are equally high. Identifying startups with high potential requires thorough research, financial analysis, and market evaluation—tasks that can be time-intensive and prone to human error. This is where artificial intelligence (AI) becomes a game-changer. AI-driven analytics enable angel investors to evaluate startups with precision, identify promising opportunities, and mitigate risks effectively.

This chapter explores how AI tools can revolutionize angel investing by analyzing startup performance, predicting success, and automating due diligence processes. Whether you're an experienced investor or new to angel investing, leveraging AI can give you a competitive edge.

1. The Role of AI in Angel Investing

1.1 Why Use AI for Angel Investing?

- **Data-Driven Decisions**: AI processes large datasets to uncover patterns and trends that humans might miss.
- **Predictive Insights**: Machine learning models forecast the likelihood of a startup's success.
- **Efficiency**: AI reduces the time spent on due diligence and market research.

1.2 Benefits of AI in Angel Investing

- **Enhanced Decision-Making**: AI provides actionable insights into a startup's potential.
- **Risk Mitigation**: Identifies red flags early, reducing the likelihood of bad investments.
- **Scalability**: Allows investors to evaluate more opportunities without increasing effort.

2. Identifying High-Potential Startups Using AI
2.1 Startup Scoring Systems

AI platforms assign scores to startups based on financial health, market conditions, and team strength:

- **EquityNet**: Uses AI to evaluate business plans and financial data, assigning risk scores to startups.
    - **Use Case**: Compare startups based on their likelihood of success.
- **Gust**: An AI-powered platform that analyzes startups' market potential and team capabilities.
    - **Use Case**: Discover vetted startups with high growth potential.

2.2 Analyzing Market Trends with AI

- **CB Insights**: Uses machine learning to analyze industry trends and identify high-growth sectors.
    - **Use Case**: Invest in startups operating in emerging markets with significant potential.
- **Crunchbase Pro**: Tracks funding rounds, market dynamics, and competitor activities.
    - **Use Case**: Identify startups gaining traction in competitive industries.

2.3 Evaluating Founding Teams

- **Pymetrics**: AI assesses founders' personalities and leadership qualities.
    - **Use Case**: Predict how effectively a team can execute their business plan.

3. AI-Driven Predictive Analytics for Startups
3.1 Predicting Startup Success

AI predicts a startup's future performance by analyzing:

- Financial metrics like revenue growth, burn rate, and profit margins.
- Product-market fit through customer reviews and feedback.
- Competitive positioning using market share data.

3.2 Key AI Tools for Predictive Analytics

- **SignalFire**: Tracks talent movements, funding patterns, and market signals to predict startup success.
    - **Use Case**: Identify early-stage startups poised for exponential growth.

- **Mattermark**: Provides growth signals based on web traffic, employee counts, and social media engagement.
    - **Use Case**: Evaluate a startup's traction before committing to investment.

4. Automating Due Diligence with AI

4.1 What is Due Diligence?

Due diligence involves verifying a startup's financial, legal, and operational status. AI streamlines this process by automating data collection and analysis.

4.2 Tools for Automating Due Diligence

- **Legalist**: Uses AI to analyze legal documents for risks and inconsistencies.
    - **Use Case**: Identify potential legal issues before investing.
- **DocuSign Insight**: AI-powered contract analysis tool for evaluating partnership agreements and obligations.
    - **Use Case**: Ensure compliance and identify red flags in agreements.

4.3 Real-Time Financial Analysis

- **Kensho**: Uses AI to analyze financial statements and market trends in real-time.
    - **Use Case**: Assess a startup's financial viability quickly and accurately.

5. AI for Risk Management in Angel Investing

5.1 Assessing Risk Factors

AI identifies risks by analyzing:

- Competitive threats.
- Regulatory challenges.
- Financial vulnerabilities.

5.2 Diversifying Investments with AI

- AI tools like **Wealthfront** recommend diversification strategies to balance risk and reward.
    - **Use Case**: Allocate funds across multiple startups in different industries.

5.3 Monitoring Post-Investment Performance

- **Tracxn**: Tracks startups' post-investment performance using AI.
    - **Use Case**: Monitor growth metrics and pivot strategies when necessary.

6. Finding Opportunities in Emerging Sectors with AI

6.1 Identifying Trends Early

AI tools like **CB Insights** and **Quid** analyze vast datasets to identify nascent trends and opportunities.

- **Example**: Discover early opportunities in industries like blockchain, green energy, or AI itself.

6.2 Evaluating Market Gaps

- **Nexla**: AI-powered data platform that identifies underserved market segments.
  - **Use Case**: Invest in startups addressing unmet consumer needs.

7. AI in Portfolio Management

7.1 Managing Multiple Investments

- **AngelList Syndicates**: Uses AI to track and manage a portfolio of angel investments.
  - **Use Case**: Monitor performance and reallocate resources dynamically.

7.2 Optimizing Returns with AI

- AI tools like **BlackRock Aladdin** optimize portfolio allocations based on risk tolerance and market conditions.
  - **Use Case**: Maximize returns by balancing high-risk and low-risk investments.

8. Ethical Considerations in AI-Driven Angel Investing

8.1 Data Privacy

- Ensure compliance with GDPR and similar regulations when analyzing startups' data.

8.2 Avoiding Algorithmic Bias

- Regularly audit AI systems to ensure fairness in evaluating startups and founders.

8.3 Transparency in Decision-Making

- Maintain transparency with startups about how AI evaluations are conducted.

9. Challenges and Limitations of AI in Angel Investing

- **Over-Reliance on Data**: AI models are only as good as the data they analyze. Incomplete or biased data can lead to inaccurate predictions.
- **Human Judgment is Irreplaceable**: AI can provide insights, but human intuition and experience remain critical.
- **Rapid Market Changes**: AI models must be updated frequently to adapt to changing market conditions.

10. Future Trends in AI for Angel Investing

- **AI-Powered Crowdfunding**: Platforms that use AI to match investors with startups based on preferences.
- **Blockchain and AI Integration**: Smart contracts for transparent and secure investment deals.
- **Real-Time Market Adaptation**: AI systems that adapt to global economic changes in real-time.

Conclusion: Mastering Angel Investing with AI

AI has transformed angel investing by providing powerful tools for analyzing startups, predicting success, and managing portfolios. By integrating AI into your investment strategy, you can reduce risks, identify high-potential opportunities, and maximize returns.

The key to successful angel investing lies in balancing AI-driven insights with human judgment and maintaining ethical practices. With the strategies and tools outlined in this chapter, you're equipped to navigate the dynamic world of startup investing and achieve financial success in the AI-powered investment era.

Part 5: AI in Personal Wealth Management

Chapter 17: AI for Tax and Financial Planning

Introduction: Automating Financial Success with AI

Tax and financial planning are essential elements of personal and business success. Traditionally, these tasks involve complex calculations, meticulous documentation, and strategic forecasting. With artificial intelligence (AI), the landscape of financial management has transformed, enabling individuals and businesses to automate processes, optimize tax filings, and maximize returns.

In this chapter, we'll explore how AI tools can streamline tax and financial planning. From automating bookkeeping to identifying tax deductions, AI makes financial management efficient, accurate, and accessible. Whether you're managing personal finances or running a business, AI offers tools and strategies to achieve financial clarity and long-term growth.

1. The Role of AI in Tax and Financial Planning

1.1 How AI Enhances Financial Management

AI simplifies financial planning by:

- Automating routine tasks like data entry and expense tracking.
- Providing real-time insights into spending, saving, and investing.
- Identifying tax deductions and credits automatically.

1.2 Benefits of AI in Tax and Financial Planning

- **Efficiency**: Reduces time spent on manual tasks.
- **Accuracy**: Minimizes errors in calculations and filings.
- **Optimization**: Identifies opportunities to save money and maximize returns.
- **Accessibility**: Makes sophisticated financial tools available to non-experts.

2. AI Tools for Automating Financial Management

2.1 Personal Finance Tools

- **Mint**: Uses AI to track spending, set budgets, and manage financial goals.
    - **Use Case**: Gain insights into personal spending habits and savings opportunities.
- **YNAB (You Need A Budget)**: AI-powered budgeting tool that forecasts cash flow.
    - **Use Case**: Plan monthly expenses and avoid overspending.
- **PocketSmith**: AI-driven tool for financial forecasting.
    - **Use Case**: Predict long-term financial outcomes based on current trends.

2.2 Business Financial Tools

- **QuickBooks AI**: Automates bookkeeping, invoicing, and expense tracking for businesses.
    - **Use Case**: Streamline accounting tasks and generate real-time financial reports.

- **Xero**: An AI-driven accounting software that integrates with bank accounts and payment systems.
    - **Use Case**: Reconcile transactions and monitor cash flow automatically.

3. AI in Tax Preparation and Filing
3.1 Automating Tax Calculations

- **TurboTax AI**: Identifies deductions and credits automatically while guiding users through the filing process.
    - **Use Case**: Simplify personal tax filing with step-by-step assistance.
- **H&R Block AI**: Offers a combination of AI tools and human expertise for accurate tax preparation.
    - **Use Case**: Handle complex tax situations with ease.

3.2 Identifying Tax Deductions

- AI analyzes expenses to identify deductible items based on tax laws:
    - **Keeper Tax**: Automatically scans receipts and expenses to find tax write-offs for freelancers and small business owners.
        - **Use Case**: Maximize tax savings without extensive record-keeping.
    - **Bench Tax**: Combines AI with bookkeeping to track deductible expenses year-round.

3.3 Handling Tax Compliance

- **Avalara**: Automates sales tax calculations and compliance for businesses.
    - **Use Case**: Ensure accurate tax reporting across multiple jurisdictions.
- **TaxJar**: AI-powered platform for managing sales tax filings and payments.
    - **Use Case**: Simplify tax compliance for e-commerce businesses.

4. Financial Forecasting with AI
4.1 Predicting Future Finances
AI uses historical data to project future trends:

- **Tiller Money**: Integrates with spreadsheets to forecast cash flow and savings goals.
    - **Use Case**: Visualize the impact of financial decisions on long-term goals.
- **Personal Capital**: Offers AI-driven tools to analyze investments and retirement plans.
    - **Use Case**: Optimize retirement savings with real-time portfolio insights.

4.2 Scenario Analysis
AI models simulate different financial scenarios to help with decision-making:

- **Zillow AI**: Projects real estate investment outcomes based on market trends.
  - **Use Case**: Assess whether buying a property aligns with financial goals.
- **PlanGuru**: Provides forecasting tools for small businesses, including "what-if" scenarios.
  - **Use Case**: Plan for potential revenue fluctuations.

5. Investment Planning with AI
5.1 Robo-Advisors
AI-powered platforms automate investment strategies:

- **Betterment**: Provides personalized investment portfolios based on risk tolerance and goals.
  - **Use Case**: Build a diversified portfolio without requiring investment expertise.
- **Wealthfront**: Uses AI to manage investments and optimize tax-loss harvesting.
  - **Use Case**: Maximize after-tax returns with automated strategies.

5.2 Real-Time Market Insights

- **Morningstar AI**: Analyzes market trends and offers actionable investment advice.
  - **Use Case**: Identify high-potential investment opportunities.
- **Acorns**: Automates micro-investments by rounding up purchases and investing the spare change.
  - **Use Case**: Build wealth passively over time.

6. AI for Debt Management
6.1 Tracking and Managing Debt

- **Debt Payoff Planner**: AI helps prioritize debt repayment strategies.
  - **Use Case**: Choose between snowball or avalanche methods for reducing debt.
- **Credit Karma**: Offers AI-driven recommendations for managing credit and improving scores.
  - **Use Case**: Identify areas for improving financial health.

6.2 Refinancing and Loan Optimization

- **LendingTree AI**: Compares loan options and predicts the best refinancing opportunities.
  - **Use Case**: Lower interest rates and monthly payments with tailored recommendations.

7. Tax and Financial Planning for Businesses

7.1 Cash Flow Management

- **Float**: AI forecasts cash flow for businesses, identifying potential shortfalls.
  - **Use Case**: Ensure liquidity for operations and investments.

7.2 Tax Optimization Strategies

- **AI Tax Consultants**: Platforms like **EY TaxChat** provide AI-enhanced tax advice.
  - **Use Case**: Optimize tax planning for long-term savings.

7.3 Compliance and Auditing

- **BlackLine**: Automates financial reconciliation and auditing processes.
  - **Use Case**: Ensure compliance with regulatory standards.

8. Challenges and Ethical Considerations

8.1 Data Security

- Protect sensitive financial information by using secure platforms and encryption.

8.2 Over-Reliance on AI

- Human oversight remains essential to validate AI-driven recommendations.

8.3 Bias and Accuracy

- Regularly audit AI models to ensure they remain unbiased and up-to-date with tax laws.

9. Future Trends in AI for Tax and Financial Planning

- **Real-Time Tax Filing**: AI systems that file taxes instantly as transactions occur.
- **Blockchain Integration**: Enhancing transparency and accuracy in financial records.
- **Predictive Financial Wellness**: AI tools offering proactive suggestions to improve financial health.

Conclusion: Achieving Financial Excellence with AI

AI is revolutionizing tax and financial planning by automating tasks, optimizing strategies, and providing real-time insights. These tools make complex processes accessible, allowing individuals and businesses to focus on growth rather than paperwork.

By integrating the tools and strategies outlined in this chapter, you can streamline your finances, reduce stress during tax season, and maximize returns year-round. AI is not just a tool—it's a partner in achieving financial success.

Chapter 18: AI-Driven Time Management

Introduction: The Value of Time in Wealth Generation

Time is one of the most valuable resources in life and business. Proper time management can be the difference between success and mediocrity, especially when the goal is wealth generation. Artificial intelligence (AI) has introduced tools that not only help manage time but also optimize productivity by automating tasks, prioritizing activities, and identifying inefficiencies. By leveraging AI-driven time management tools, individuals and businesses can focus on high-value activities that directly contribute to financial success.

This chapter explores how AI can help you reclaim your time, boost productivity, and create opportunities for wealth generation. From automating routine tasks to personalizing schedules, AI tools are transforming how we manage our days.

1. The Importance of AI in Time Management

1.1 Why AI is a Game-Changer for Time Management

- **Automation**: AI eliminates repetitive tasks, freeing up time for strategic thinking.
- **Prioritization**: AI tools analyze tasks and recommend the most critical ones to focus on.
- **Personalization**: AI creates schedules tailored to individual productivity patterns.

1.2 Benefits of AI-Driven Time Management

- **Increased Productivity**: Focus on high-value tasks that maximize output.
- **Stress Reduction**: Simplify decision-making and reduce mental load.
- **Better Work-Life Balance**: Free up time for personal pursuits and wealth-building activities.

2. AI Tools for Task Management and Automation

2.1 Automating Routine Tasks

- **Zapier**: Connects apps and automates workflows across platforms.
    - **Use Case**: Automatically send follow-up emails or update project management tools after task completion.
- **IFTTT (If This Then That)**: Automates actions between devices and apps.
    - **Use Case**: Sync calendar events with reminders or trigger notifications for key tasks.

2.2 Organizing and Prioritizing Tasks

- **Todoist with AI**: Prioritizes tasks based on deadlines, importance, and user-defined criteria.
    - **Use Case**: Focus on critical tasks without manually organizing your to-do list.
- **Notion AI**: Combines note-taking, project management, and task prioritization in a single platform.
    - **Use Case**: Create dynamic workflows that adapt to your evolving priorities.

2.3 Virtual Assistants

- **Microsoft Cortana**: Automates scheduling and sends reminders for upcoming tasks.
    - **Use Case**: Simplify calendar management and ensure timely task execution.
- **Google Assistant**: Manages reminders, schedules, and integrations with other apps.
    - **Use Case**: Automate personal and professional time management.

3. AI-Powered Scheduling and Calendar Optimization

3.1 Intelligent Scheduling

- **Clockwise**: Optimizes your calendar by identifying blocks of focused work time.
    - **Use Case**: Minimize meeting disruptions and maximize deep work periods.
- **TimeHero**: Automatically schedules tasks based on priorities and deadlines.
    - **Use Case**: Ensure every task is allocated adequate time without manual planning.

3.2 Meeting Management

- **X.AI**: An AI scheduling assistant that arranges meetings and avoids conflicts.
    - **Use Case**: Automate meeting scheduling and save hours of back-and-forth emails.
- **Otter.ai**: Provides AI-generated meeting transcriptions and highlights key points.
    - **Use Case**: Review meetings quickly without taking detailed notes.

3.3 Predictive Planning

- **Trevor AI**: Syncs tasks with your calendar and predicts the best times to complete them.
    - **Use Case**: Balance workloads by distributing tasks evenly throughout the week.

4. Optimizing Productivity with AI
4.1 Analyzing Productivity Patterns

- **RescueTime**: Tracks time spent on apps, websites, and tasks to identify productivity trends.
    - **Use Case**: Pinpoint time-wasting activities and focus on productive habits.
- **Focus@Will**: Uses AI to recommend music that boosts focus and efficiency.
    - **Use Case**: Create a distraction-free environment for deep work.

4.2 Managing Focus and Breaks

- **Serene**: An AI-driven tool that promotes focus by blocking distractions and scheduling breaks.
    - **Use Case**: Maintain peak productivity without burnout.
- **Flow App**: Implements the Pomodoro Technique with AI insights for timing work sessions.
    - **Use Case**: Break large tasks into manageable intervals for sustained focus.

4.3 Workflow Automation

- **Monday.com with AI**: Automates project workflows, tracks progress, and predicts bottlenecks.
    - **Use Case**: Ensure seamless collaboration and project execution.
- **Asana AI**: Suggests task assignments and timelines based on team performance.
    - **Use Case**: Delegate tasks effectively and stay ahead of deadlines.

5. Freeing Up Time for Wealth Generation
5.1 Automating Financial Management

- **QuickBooks AI**: Manages invoicing, expense tracking, and financial reporting.
    - **Use Case**: Save hours on bookkeeping and focus on business growth.
- **YNAB (You Need A Budget)**: Tracks budgets and identifies savings opportunities.
    - **Use Case**: Allocate savings toward investments or business ventures.

5.2 Delegating with AI

- **Scribe AI**: Automates documentation and process creation for repetitive tasks.
    - **Use Case**: Delegate operational tasks to virtual assistants or team members.
- **RPA Tools (Robotic Process Automation)**: Automates repetitive tasks across departments.
    - **Use Case**: Focus on strategic decision-making by delegating routine operations to AI bots.

5.3 Scaling Productivity for Passive Income Streams

- Use AI tools like **Shopify AI** or **Gumroad AI** to automate e-commerce and digital product management.
    - **Use Case**: Free up time for creating new income-generating opportunities.

6. AI-Driven Decision Making

6.1 Prioritizing Goals with AI

- **Compass AI**: Aligns tasks with long-term objectives.
    - **Use Case**: Ensure daily efforts contribute directly to financial and personal goals.
- **ClickUp AI**: Analyzes team productivity and recommends optimizations.
    - **Use Case**: Improve team performance while focusing on wealth-building initiatives.

6.2 Scenario Analysis and Forecasting

- **PlanRadar**: Uses AI to simulate project outcomes and allocate resources efficiently.
    - **Use Case**: Anticipate resource needs for time-sensitive projects.

7. Overcoming Time Management Challenges with AI

7.1 Avoiding Over-Scheduling

AI tools like **Clockwise** analyze workload distribution and suggest adjustments to prevent burnout.

7.2 Managing Interruptions

- **Freedom**: Blocks distracting websites and apps during work hours.
    - **Use Case**: Stay focused on high-priority tasks.

7.3 Balancing Automation with Human Input

AI should complement, not replace, human decision-making. Use tools like **Notion AI** to provide context for automation decisions.

8. Ethical Considerations in AI Time Management

8.1 Privacy Concerns

- Ensure tools comply with data protection regulations like GDPR and CCPA.

8.2 Avoiding Over-Reliance on AI

- Maintain a balance between AI-driven recommendations and personal judgment.

8.3 Ensuring Fair Use

- Encourage transparency in how AI systems prioritize and allocate tasks.

9. Future Trends in AI-Driven Time Management

- **AI-Powered Wearables**: Devices that monitor productivity and suggest adjustments in real-time.
- **Integrated Life Assistants**: AI systems that coordinate personal and professional schedules seamlessly.
- **Adaptive Learning Algorithms**: Tools that evolve with user behavior for increasingly personalized time management.

Conclusion: Reclaiming Time with AI for Wealth Generation

AI has revolutionized time management, enabling individuals and businesses to optimize productivity and focus on high-value activities. By automating routine tasks, prioritizing goals, and analyzing productivity patterns, AI empowers you to make the most of your time.

The strategies and tools outlined in this chapter provide a roadmap for using AI to create more free time and channel it into wealth-generating endeavors. Remember, time is your most valuable asset, and with AI as your partner, you can achieve unparalleled efficiency and success.

Chapter 19: Building Personal Brands with AI

Introduction: Leveraging AI to Shape Your Public Image

In today's digital age, building a personal brand is essential for professionals, entrepreneurs, and creatives seeking to establish credibility, influence, and success. Your personal brand reflects who you are, what you stand for, and the value you bring to your audience. Artificial intelligence (AI) has revolutionized personal branding by offering tools to craft, amplify, and manage your public image with precision and efficiency.

This chapter delves into how AI can help you create a compelling personal brand, streamline content creation, manage your online presence, and engage with your audience authentically. Whether you're a business leader, content creator, or aspiring influencer, AI tools and strategies can help you stand out in an increasingly competitive landscape.

1. Understanding Personal Branding with AI

1.1 What is Personal Branding?

Personal branding is the process of defining and promoting your unique identity, expertise, and values to a target audience. Key elements include:

- **Authenticity**: Showcasing your genuine personality and values.
- **Expertise**: Highlighting your knowledge and skills.
- **Relevance**: Engaging with an audience that aligns with your goals.

1.2 The Role of AI in Personal Branding

AI simplifies and enhances the personal branding process by:

- Automating content creation and curation.
- Providing insights into audience preferences and engagement.
- Monitoring and managing your online reputation.

2. Defining Your Personal Brand with AI

2.1 Discovering Your Unique Value Proposition

AI tools can help you identify your strengths and niche:

- **Crystal Knows**: Analyzes your personality traits to craft messaging that resonates with your audience.
    - **Use Case**: Align your brand voice with your natural communication style.
- **StrengthsFinder AI**: Provides insights into your key strengths and how to position them in your personal brand.

2.2 Understanding Your Audience

AI tools analyze audience data to identify their preferences and needs:

- **SparkToro**: Discovers where your audience spends time online and what content they consume.
    - **Use Case**: Focus your branding efforts on platforms and topics that matter to your target audience.
- **Brandwatch Consumer Intelligence**: Tracks audience sentiment and trends.
    - **Use Case**: Adjust your messaging to align with audience expectations.

2.3 Crafting Your Brand Identity

- **Looka AI**: Creates professional logos and brand assets.
    - **Use Case**: Develop a cohesive visual identity for your brand.
- **Canva AI**: Designs social media templates, business cards, and presentations.
    - **Use Case**: Maintain consistent branding across platforms.

3. Content Creation with AI
3.1 Automating Written Content

- **Jasper AI (formerly Jarvis)**: Generates blog posts, captions, and email newsletters tailored to your audience.
    - **Use Case**: Publish high-quality content consistently.
- **Copy.ai**: Creates compelling copy for websites, ads, and social media posts.
    - **Use Case**: Craft engaging messages that reflect your brand voice.

3.2 Enhancing Visual Content

- **DALL·E by OpenAI**: Generates unique visuals based on text prompts.
    - **Use Case**: Stand out with custom illustrations for your social media and website.
- **Lumen5**: Converts articles and blog posts into engaging videos.
    - **Use Case**: Repurpose long-form content into visual formats for greater reach.

3.3 Video Content Creation

- **Descript**: Edits videos and podcasts using AI-driven tools.
    - **Use Case**: Create polished video content to showcase your expertise.
- **Synthesia**: Generates AI-powered video presentations featuring virtual avatars.
    - **Use Case**: Produce professional video content without requiring a studio.

4. Managing Your Online Presence with AI
4.1 Social Media Automation

- **Hootsuite with AI**: Schedules posts, analyzes performance, and suggests optimal posting times.
    - **Use Case**: Maintain a consistent presence across multiple platforms.
- **Buffer AI**: Provides content suggestions and engagement analytics.
    - **Use Case**: Improve engagement rates with data-backed content strategies.

4.2 Reputation Management

- **Brand24**: Monitors online mentions of your name or brand.
    - **Use Case**: Respond to feedback and manage your public image proactively.
- **Awario**: Tracks sentiment around your brand in real-time.
    - **Use Case**: Address negative feedback before it escalates.

4.3 SEO Optimization

- **Surfer SEO**: Optimizes website and blog content for search engines.
    - **Use Case**: Increase visibility and attract more organic traffic.
- **Ahrefs AI**: Provides keyword research and competitive analysis.
    - **Use Case**: Rank higher on search engines for terms relevant to your brand.

5. Engaging with Your Audience Using AI

5.1 Personalized Interactions

- **ManyChat**: Creates AI-driven chatbots for Facebook and Instagram.
    - **Use Case**: Answer audience queries instantly and keep them engaged.
- **Intercom with AI**: Automates customer support and personalizes communication.
    - **Use Case**: Build stronger relationships through tailored interactions.

5.2 Audience Growth and Networking

- **LinkedIn Sales Navigator AI**: Identifies potential connections and opportunities for networking.
    - **Use Case**: Expand your professional network strategically.
- **Nimble CRM**: Tracks interactions and opportunities across platforms.
    - **Use Case**: Nurture meaningful relationships with your audience.

6. Monitoring and Evolving Your Personal Brand

6.1 Tracking Metrics with AI

- **Google Analytics 4**: Measures website performance and audience behavior.
    - **Use Case**: Identify which content drives the most engagement.
- **Socialbakers AI**: Provides insights into social media performance and audience preferences.
    - **Use Case**: Refine your social media strategy based on real-time data.

6.2 Adapting to Trends

- **BuzzSumo**: Identifies trending topics and content relevant to your audience.
    - **Use Case**: Stay ahead by creating content on emerging trends.
- **Trendspottr**: Uses AI to forecast future trends in your niche.
    - **Use Case**: Position your brand as a thought leader in your industry.

7. Monetizing Your Personal Brand with AI

7.1 Digital Products and Services

- Use AI tools like **Teachable AI** to create and market online courses.
  - **Use Case**: Turn your expertise into a passive income stream.

7.2 Collaborations and Sponsorships

- **AspireIQ**: Connects influencers with brands for partnerships.
  - **Use Case**: Monetize your personal brand through collaborations.

7.3 Content Monetization

- **Patreon AI Tools**: Automates membership management for exclusive content.
  - **Use Case**: Earn directly from your audience by offering premium content.

8. Ethical Considerations in AI-Driven Personal Branding

8.1 Authenticity vs. Automation

- Ensure AI tools enhance, not replace, your genuine voice and personality.

8.2 Data Privacy

- Use platforms compliant with data regulations like GDPR and CCPA to protect your audience's information.

8.3 Addressing Bias

- Regularly review AI-generated content to ensure inclusivity and fairness.

9. Future Trends in AI and Personal Branding

- **Hyper-Personalized Branding**: AI tools offering deeper audience segmentation and individualized strategies.
- **AR and VR Integration**: Augmented reality experiences to showcase your brand in innovative ways.
- **Voice AI and Personal Branding**: Leveraging voice assistants and podcasts for brand expansion.

Conclusion: Building a Standout Personal Brand with AI

AI has transformed personal branding from a manual, time-intensive process into a streamlined, data-driven strategy. By leveraging AI tools, you can define your brand, create engaging content, and connect authentically with your audience.

The strategies outlined in this chapter empower you to craft a personal brand that resonates, inspires, and drives success. Remember, your personal brand is an ongoing journey, and with AI as your ally, you can adapt, grow, and thrive in the digital age.

Part 6: Expanding Beyond the Limits

Chapter 20: AI in Education: Learning Your Way to Wealth

Introduction: The Power of AI in Learning and Wealth Creation

Education is the cornerstone of success and wealth generation. In a rapidly evolving world, staying relevant requires continuous learning and skill development. Artificial intelligence (AI) has emerged as a transformative force in education, enabling personalized learning, automating tedious tasks, and providing real-time insights into skill development. By harnessing AI, learners can accelerate their knowledge acquisition and position themselves for financial success in competitive industries.

This chapter explores how AI-driven tools and strategies can empower individuals to learn faster, develop in-demand skills, and unlock opportunities for wealth creation. Whether you're advancing your career, building a business, or exploring new fields, AI can be your most powerful educational ally.

1. The Role of AI in Education and Skill Development

1.1 How AI Enhances Learning

AI tailors educational content to individual needs, ensuring a more effective learning experience:

- **Personalization**: Adapts lessons to match the learner's pace and preferences.
- **Automation**: Reduces time spent on repetitive tasks like grading and scheduling.
- **Accessibility**: Makes quality education available to learners worldwide.

1.2 Benefits of AI in Skill Development

- **Efficiency**: Accelerates learning by focusing on key areas for improvement.
- **Flexibility**: Offers on-demand access to courses and resources.
- **Relevance**: Keeps content updated with the latest industry trends and technologies.

2. AI-Powered Learning Platforms

2.1 Personalized Learning Platforms

- **Duolingo AI**: Offers adaptive language learning based on user progress and mistakes.
  - **Use Case**: Quickly acquire new languages for global business opportunities.
- **Khan Academy with AI**: Provides personalized lesson plans and real-time feedback.
  - **Use Case**: Master foundational skills like math, finance, and economics.

2.2 Skill Development Platforms

- **Coursera with AI**: Suggests courses tailored to career goals and learning history.
  - **Use Case**: Gain certifications in high-demand fields like AI, data science, and business.
- **Udemy AI**: Analyzes user preferences to recommend relevant courses.
  - **Use Case**: Explore niche topics for entrepreneurial or career growth.

2.3 AI-Driven Microlearning Tools

- **EdApp**: Breaks lessons into bite-sized modules for quick learning.
  - **Use Case**: Learn essential skills during short breaks in your day.
- **Blinkist**: Summarizes books and key concepts in under 15 minutes.
  - **Use Case**: Absorb business insights and strategies from bestselling books.

3. Accelerating Knowledge Acquisition with AI

3.1 Adaptive Learning Systems

- **Socratic by Google**: AI answers questions and explains concepts with step-by-step solutions.
  - **Use Case**: Clarify complex topics in real-time.
- **ALEKS (Assessment and Learning in Knowledge Spaces)**: Adapts content based on your knowledge gaps.
  - **Use Case**: Strengthen weak areas for a comprehensive understanding of subjects.

3.2 Real-Time Feedback and Assessment

- **Grammarly with AI**: Improves writing skills by offering instant suggestions and feedback.
  - **Use Case**: Enhance communication skills crucial for business and networking.
- **CodeSignal**: Assesses coding skills and offers improvement suggestions.
  - **Use Case**: Prepare for technical interviews or build programming expertise.

3.3 AI-Powered Research Tools

- **ResearchRabbit**: Helps users discover and organize academic papers efficiently.
    - **Use Case**: Stay informed about trends and innovations in your field.
- **Semantic Scholar**: Uses AI to recommend research papers relevant to your interests.
    - **Use Case**: Dive deeper into specialized knowledge areas.

4. Building In-Demand Skills for Wealth Creation

4.1 Identifying High-Demand Skills with AI

- **LinkedIn Learning with AI**: Tracks job market trends and suggests skills to develop.
    - **Use Case**: Focus on emerging skills like AI, cybersecurity, or blockchain.
- **Burning Glass Technologies**: Analyzes job postings to identify future skill demands.
    - **Use Case**: Align your learning with market opportunities.

4.2 Learning Financial Literacy

- **Zogo Finance**: Gamifies financial education using AI to make learning engaging.
    - **Use Case**: Master budgeting, investing, and financial planning.
- **Morningstar Investor**: Offers AI-driven insights for understanding investments.
    - **Use Case**: Build wealth by learning to manage and grow your portfolio.

4.3 Mastering Business Skills

- **Skillshare AI**: Offers courses on entrepreneurship, leadership, and marketing.
    - **Use Case**: Develop skills essential for launching and managing a business.
- **HubSpot Academy with AI**: Provides free marketing, sales, and customer service training.
    - **Use Case**: Enhance your digital marketing expertise for personal branding or business growth.

5. AI for Continuous Professional Development
5.1 Certification and Credentialing

- **Google Career Certificates**: AI-driven courses provide job-ready skills and certifications.
  - **Use Case**: Transition into fields like IT, project management, or data analysis.
- **Credly**: Uses AI to validate skills and issue digital badges.
  - **Use Case**: Showcase verified expertise to potential employers or clients.

5.2 Corporate Training with AI

- **Degreed**: Tracks employees' learning progress and suggests resources.
  - **Use Case**: Stay competitive in your industry with ongoing skill upgrades.
- **EdCast**: AI curates personalized learning paths for professionals.
  - **Use Case**: Accelerate career advancement by mastering new technologies.

6. Leveraging AI for Entrepreneurial Learning
6.1 Starting and Scaling a Business

- **StartUp.ai**: AI-based platform offering guidance on business planning and growth strategies.
  - **Use Case**: Learn how to develop a successful business model.
- **Bizplan**: Uses AI to simplify business plan creation and financial forecasting.
  - **Use Case**: Turn your ideas into actionable plans for wealth creation.

6.2 Networking and Collaboration

- **Shapr AI**: Suggests professional connections based on shared interests and goals.
  - **Use Case**: Build a network of mentors, investors, and collaborators.
- **Lunchclub**: Uses AI to match users with professionals for meaningful networking.
  - **Use Case**: Explore partnerships and business opportunities.

7. AI in Self-Paced and Collaborative Learning
7.1 AI for Self-Paced Learning

- **Brilliant.org**: Interactive AI-driven lessons in STEM and finance.
  - **Use Case**: Learn at your own pace while mastering challenging concepts.
- **Knewton**: Adapts content delivery to match individual learning styles.
  - **Use Case**: Maximize comprehension and retention of material.

7.2 Collaborative Learning Platforms

- **Discord AI Bots**: Facilitate study groups and collaborative learning sessions.
  - **Use Case**: Share knowledge and solve problems with peers in real-time.
- **Piazza AI**: Enhances online classroom discussions and knowledge-sharing.
  - **Use Case**: Engage in interactive learning with a global community.

8. Monitoring Progress and Measuring Success
8.1 AI for Tracking Learning Outcomes

- **Learning Locker**: Tracks learning data to measure progress and impact.
  - **Use Case**: Identify areas for improvement and celebrate milestones.
- **CanopyLAB**: Provides insights into your learning journey and skill development.
  - **Use Case**: Align progress with career goals.

8.2 Gamifying Education with AI

- **Kahoot! AI**: Makes learning fun and interactive with quizzes and challenges.
  - **Use Case**: Retain knowledge through engaging gamified experiences.

9. Ethical and Practical Considerations in AI-Driven Education

9.1 Addressing Data Privacy

- Ensure that platforms comply with GDPR and CCPA regulations.

9.2 Avoiding Over-Reliance on AI

- Combine AI-driven learning with hands-on practice and human interaction.

9.3 Ensuring Accessibility

- Promote equitable access to AI-powered education for underserved communities.

10. Future Trends in AI and Education

- **Immersive Learning with AI and VR**: AI-driven virtual reality environments for hands-on learning experiences.
- **AI Tutors**: Personalized virtual tutors that provide 24/7 support.
- **Lifelong Learning Platforms**: AI systems that evolve with users' careers and changing skill demands.

Conclusion: Accelerating Knowledge for Wealth Creation

AI has made education more accessible, personalized, and impactful. By leveraging AI tools, you can accelerate your learning, acquire in-demand skills, and position yourself for financial success. The strategies outlined in this chapter empower you to turn knowledge into wealth, whether through advancing your career, building a business, or mastering financial literacy.

In the age of AI, learning is not just a tool for personal growth—it's a gateway to limitless opportunities. Embrace AI in education to unlock your full potential and achieve your wealth-building goals.

Chapter 21: AI-Powered Social Impact

Introduction: Leveraging AI Wealth for Global Good

The transformative power of artificial intelligence (AI) extends beyond business and personal wealth; it has the potential to address some of the world's most pressing challenges. By using AI to create wealth, individuals and organizations can reinvest those resources into meaningful social impact initiatives, fostering change in areas like poverty reduction, healthcare, education, and environmental conservation. AI technologies can amplify efforts by analyzing complex problems, scaling solutions, and delivering measurable outcomes.

This chapter explores how AI-driven wealth can be strategically deployed to create positive social impact, from funding impactful projects to directly applying AI technologies for global good. It provides actionable insights for leveraging AI in philanthropy, sustainability, and community development.

1. The Potential of AI in Social Impact

1.1 Why AI is a Game-Changer for Social Impact

- **Scalability**: AI-driven solutions can be scaled globally to address large-scale issues.
- **Efficiency**: AI streamlines processes, reduces costs, and accelerates outcomes.
- **Precision**: AI uses data to pinpoint the root causes of problems and predict outcomes effectively.

1.2 Examples of AI-Powered Social Impact

- **Healthcare**: AI detecting diseases early in underserved regions.
- **Education**: Personalized learning platforms reaching remote areas.
- **Environment**: AI tracking deforestation and optimizing renewable energy use.

2. Funding Social Impact with AI-Generated Wealth

2.1 Philanthropy in the AI Age

- Use AI-generated wealth to fund impactful philanthropic initiatives:
    - **Example**: Donating proceeds from AI-powered businesses to global education programs.

2.2 Venture Philanthropy

- Combine philanthropic giving with investment strategies to support sustainable impact projects:
    - **Example**: Funding social enterprises that use AI for good, such as clean energy startups or tech-based healthcare solutions.

2.3 Crowdfunding with AI

- **GoFundMe with AI**: Automates donor targeting and campaign optimization for greater reach.
    - **Use Case**: Fund community-driven projects efficiently.
- **ImpactGuru**: Uses AI to connect donors with urgent global needs.

3. AI in Solving Global Challenges

3.1 Poverty Alleviation

- **AI in Microfinance**:
    - Platforms like **Tala** use AI to assess creditworthiness and provide microloans to underserved populations.
    - **Use Case**: Empower entrepreneurs in developing regions with access to capital.
- **Predictive Analytics for Social Programs**:
    - AI tools like **DataKind** optimize resource allocation for poverty reduction programs.

3.2 Healthcare

- **AI in Disease Prediction and Prevention**:
    - **Google's DeepMind** analyzes patient data to predict and prevent diseases like kidney failure or diabetic retinopathy.
    - **Use Case**: Improve healthcare delivery in rural areas.
- **AI-Powered Remote Diagnostics**:
    - Tools like **Ada Health** provide accessible diagnostic support via mobile apps.

3.3 Education

- **Adaptive Learning Platforms**:
    - AI-powered tools like **Khan Academy AI** deliver personalized education to underserved communities.
    - **Use Case**: Bridge the global education gap.
- **AI-Driven Language Learning**:
    - Tools like **Duolingo AI** offer free language education to help learners access better opportunities.

4. AI for Environmental Conservation
4.1 Fighting Climate Change

- **Carbon Emission Monitoring**:
  - AI tools like **Pachama** analyze carbon offsets and forest conservation efforts.
  - **Use Case**: Support reforestation projects with precise impact tracking.
- **Renewable Energy Optimization**:
  - AI systems like **Google's DeepMind Energy** optimize power grid efficiency.

4.2 Wildlife Protection

- **AI in Poaching Prevention**:
  - Tools like **PAWS (Protection Assistant for Wildlife Security)** use predictive algorithms to prevent illegal poaching.
  - **Use Case**: Protect endangered species in wildlife reserves.

4.3 Sustainable Agriculture

- **AI-Driven Farming**:
  - Platforms like **FarmLogs** analyze soil conditions, weather patterns, and crop health to improve yields sustainably.
  - **Use Case**: Increase food security in vulnerable regions.

5. Empowering Communities with AI
5.1 Smart Cities

- **AI in Urban Planning**:
  - Tools like **Sidewalk Labs** optimize transportation, energy use, and infrastructure development.
  - **Use Case**: Build sustainable and efficient urban environments.

5.2 Disaster Relief and Management

- **AI for Disaster Prediction**:
  - Systems like **IBM's Watson** predict natural disasters and streamline relief efforts.
  - **Use Case**: Reduce the impact of hurricanes, floods, and wildfires.
- **Crisis Mapping with AI**:
  - Platforms like **Ushahidi** use AI to collect real-time data during crises for effective response.

5.3 Promoting Inclusion

- **AI for Accessibility**:
    - Tools like **Seeing AI** provide visually impaired individuals with real-time assistance.
    - **Use Case**: Enhance the quality of life for people with disabilities.

6. AI-Powered Financial Inclusion

6.1 Expanding Financial Access

- AI tools like **Zest AI** analyze alternative data to provide loans to underserved communities.
    - **Use Case**: Help individuals build credit and achieve financial independence.

6.2 Blockchain and AI Integration

- **Decentralized Aid**: Blockchain-powered AI platforms ensure transparency in aid distribution.
    - **Use Case**: Prevent corruption and ensure funds reach intended beneficiaries.

7. Monitoring and Measuring Social Impact with AI

7.1 Tracking Progress

- **ImpactCloud AI**: Provides real-time analytics on social impact initiatives.
    - **Use Case**: Monitor the effectiveness of programs and adjust strategies accordingly.

7.2 Data-Driven Decision Making

- AI uses predictive analytics to forecast the long-term outcomes of social projects.

7.3 Visualizing Impact

- **Tableau with AI**: Creates dashboards to present data on social impact visually.
    - **Use Case**: Communicate results to stakeholders effectively.

8. Challenges and Ethical Considerations

8.1 Bias in AI Systems

- Ensure that AI algorithms are audited regularly to prevent bias in decision-making.

8.2 Data Privacy

- Use platforms that comply with data protection regulations like GDPR and CCPA.

8.3 Equitable Access to AI

- Address the digital divide by ensuring marginalized communities benefit from AI solutions.

9. Future Trends in AI-Powered Social Impact

- **AI-Driven Policy Making**: Governments using AI to create evidence-based social policies.
- **Global AI Collaborations**: Partnerships between nations to address shared challenges like climate change.
- **AI in Universal Basic Income**: Automated systems for equitable income distribution.

Conclusion: Transforming the World with AI Wealth

AI is not just a tool for personal and organizational growth; it's a catalyst for global transformation. By using AI to generate wealth and reinvesting it into social impact initiatives, individuals and organizations can address pressing global challenges and create a more equitable and sustainable future.

The strategies outlined in this chapter empower you to align your financial success with meaningful contributions to society. By embracing AI for social impact, you can become a driving force for positive change in the world.

Chapter 22: AI and Future-Proof Industries

Introduction: AI's Role in Shaping the Industries of Tomorrow

Artificial intelligence (AI) is no longer just a tool for optimizing processes; it is a transformative force reshaping entire industries. From healthcare and finance to retail and logistics, AI is disrupting traditional business models, creating new opportunities, and rendering some roles obsolete. For investors, entrepreneurs, and professionals, understanding which industries are poised for massive AI disruption is critical for staying ahead of the curve and future-proofing their endeavors.

This chapter explores industries that are being revolutionized by AI and identifies opportunities for wealth creation, career advancement, and innovative solutions.

1. Characteristics of Future-Proof Industries

1.1 Industries that Leverage AI's Core Strengths

Industries with large datasets, repetitive processes, and high demand for efficiency are ripe for AI disruption.

- **Key Characteristics**:
  - Heavy reliance on data analysis.
  - Processes that can be automated.
  - High potential for cost savings and scalability.

1.2 Indicators of AI-Driven Growth

- Increasing AI adoption rates.
- Significant investment in AI research and development.
- Emergence of AI-driven startups disrupting traditional markets.

2. Healthcare: AI Revolutionizing Medical Science

2.1 Precision Medicine

AI tools like **DeepMind** and **IBM Watson Health** analyze genetic data and medical histories to tailor treatments.

- **Opportunities**:
    - AI-driven drug discovery.
    - Personalized healthcare plans.
    - Early disease detection tools.

2.2 Remote Diagnostics and Telemedicine

- **Tools**: **Ada Health**, **Babylon Health**.
    - **Use Case**: AI-powered apps that provide instant diagnoses based on symptoms.

2.3 Robotic Surgery

AI enhances precision and minimizes risks during surgeries.

- **Example**: **da Vinci Surgical System** integrating AI for better outcomes.

2.4 AI in Mental Health

- **Tools**: **Woebot**, **Replika** provide AI-powered therapy and mental health support.
    - **Opportunities**: Expand mental health accessibility globally.

3. Finance: The AI-Driven Fintech Boom

3.1 Algorithmic Trading

AI systems predict market trends and execute trades with minimal human intervention.

- **Tools**: **Kavout**, **QuantConnect**.
    - **Opportunities**: Build AI-driven investment portfolios.

3.2 Fraud Detection and Risk Management

AI detects fraudulent transactions in real time.

- **Examples**: **FICO Falcon**, **Zest AI**.
    - **Opportunities**: Create fraud prevention platforms for niche markets.

3.3 Personalized Banking

- **Tools**: AI chatbots like **Erica** by Bank of America offer personalized banking advice.
    - **Opportunities**: Develop AI-driven financial planning apps.

4. Retail: Transforming the Consumer Experience

4.1 Personalized Shopping Experiences

AI algorithms recommend products tailored to individual preferences.

- **Examples**: **Amazon's AI-driven recommendations**, **Dynamic Yield**.

4.2 Supply Chain Optimization

AI predicts demand and manages inventory efficiently.

- **Tools**: **Blue Yonder**, **SAP Integrated Business Planning**.
    - **Opportunities**: Invest in AI platforms that optimize supply chains.

4.3 Autonomous Retail Stores

- **Examples**: Amazon Go's cashier-less stores use AI for seamless shopping experiences.

4.4 Visual Search and AR

- **Tools**: AI-powered visual search platforms like **Syte**.
    - **Opportunities**: Develop AI-driven AR solutions for retail.

5. Transportation and Logistics: AI Driving Efficiency

5.1 Autonomous Vehicles

- **Leaders**: Tesla, Waymo, and Cruise are at the forefront of self-driving technology.
    - **Opportunities**: Invest in AI-powered logistics and fleet management startups.

5.2 Route Optimization

- **Tools**: **Onfleet AI**, **ClearMetal**.
    - **Use Case**: Real-time optimization of delivery routes.

5.3 Warehouse Automation

- **Examples**: AI robots by **Boston Dynamics** and **Kiva Systems** manage warehouse logistics.

6. Education: AI Empowering Personalized Learning

6.1 Adaptive Learning Platforms

- **Examples**: **Coursera, Khan Academy AI** adapt courses to individual learning speeds.
    - **Opportunities**: Build niche educational platforms tailored to underserved demographics.

6.2 AI-Powered Tutoring

- **Tools**: **Socratic by Google, Duolingo AI**.
    - **Use Case**: Deliver affordable, high-quality tutoring worldwide.

6.3 Skill Gap Analysis

AI identifies skill gaps in employees and recommends training.

- **Examples**: **Degreed, Skillsoft**.

7. Agriculture: Smarter Farming with AI

7.1 Precision Agriculture

AI optimizes crop yields by analyzing soil conditions and weather patterns.

- **Tools**: **FarmLogs, Taranis**.

7.2 Automated Farming Equipment

- **Examples**: John Deere's AI-powered tractors.
    - **Opportunities**: Develop affordable AI solutions for small-scale farmers.

7.3 Food Supply Chain Management

AI predicts demand and reduces waste.

- **Tools**: **IBM Food Trust**.

8. Energy: The AI Revolution in Sustainability

8.1 Renewable Energy Optimization

AI manages renewable energy grids efficiently.

- **Examples**: **Google DeepMind's Energy AI**.

8.2 Predictive Maintenance

AI predicts equipment failures in power plants.

- **Tools**: **Uptake AI**, **SparkCognition**.

8.3 Smart Grid Management

AI balances supply and demand in real time.

- **Use Case**: Build smarter energy systems for urban areas.

9. Entertainment and Media: AI Creating Immersive Experiences

9.1 Content Creation

AI generates music, scripts, and videos.

- **Tools**: **Jukedeck**, **Runway ML**.

9.2 Personalization

Streaming platforms use AI to recommend content.

- **Examples**: Netflix, Spotify.

9.3 Gaming

AI enhances game environments and player interactions.

- **Examples**: AI-powered NPCs in open-world games.

10. Cybersecurity: Defending the Digital Frontier
10.1 Threat Detection
AI identifies and mitigates cyber threats.

- **Examples: Darktrace, CrowdStrike.**

10.2 Automated Incident Response
AI responds to attacks faster than humans.

- **Tools: IBM QRadar.**

10.3 Privacy and Data Protection
AI ensures compliance with regulations like GDPR.
11. Opportunities for Entrepreneurs and Investors
11.1 Investing in AI Startups
Identify industries where AI adoption is nascent but promising.
11.2 Developing AI Skills
Equip yourself or your workforce with AI expertise to stay competitive.
11.3 Partnering with AI Innovators
Collaborate with AI companies to integrate their solutions into existing businesses.
12. Ethical and Practical Considerations
12.1 Job Displacement

- Address workforce transitions with AI-driven upskilling programs.

12.2 Bias in AI Algorithms

- Ensure transparency and fairness in AI models.

12.3 Balancing Innovation and Regulation

- Collaborate with regulators to create ethical AI solutions.

Conclusion: Capitalizing on AI-Driven Industries

AI is disrupting industries at an unprecedented pace, offering opportunities for innovation, investment, and career growth. By identifying and engaging with future-proof industries, you can position yourself to thrive in the AI-powered economy.

The key to success lies in adaptability—embracing AI-driven changes while staying informed about trends and challenges. With the insights provided in this chapter, you are equipped to navigate the transformative landscape of AI and secure your place in the industries of tomorrow.

Chapter 23: The Role of AI in Longevity

Introduction: AI as the Key to a Longer, Healthier Life

The quest for longevity—living a longer, healthier, and more productive life—has been a central goal of human innovation. Recent advancements in artificial intelligence (AI) have accelerated progress in this area, offering transformative solutions in healthcare, nutrition, genetics, and lifestyle optimization. AI-driven technologies are unlocking the secrets of aging, identifying interventions that slow its effects, and personalizing strategies for extended lifespans.

In this chapter, we explore how AI innovations are shaping the future of longevity. From early disease detection to personalized health recommendations, AI is helping individuals live not only longer but also more fulfilling and productive lives.

1. Understanding Longevity and the Role of AI

1.1 What is Longevity?

Longevity refers to extending the human lifespan while maintaining physical and mental health. It involves delaying the onset of age-related diseases and optimizing well-being.

1.2 Why AI is a Game-Changer in Longevity Research

- **Data Analysis**: AI processes massive datasets to uncover patterns in health, aging, and disease.
- **Predictive Capabilities**: AI forecasts health outcomes based on genetic, lifestyle, and environmental factors.
- **Personalization**: AI tailors interventions to individual needs for maximum effectiveness.

2. AI-Driven Innovations in Longevity Research

2.1 AI in Genetic Research

- **CRISPR and AI**: AI optimizes gene-editing techniques like CRISPR to correct genetic mutations linked to aging and diseases.
  - **Example**: Identifying genes responsible for cellular repair and enhancing their function.

2.2 Cellular and Molecular Biology

- AI tools like **DeepMind's AlphaFold** predict protein structures critical to understanding cellular aging.
  - **Use Case**: Develop anti-aging therapies targeting cellular mechanisms.

2.3 Drug Discovery for Longevity

- **Insilico Medicine**: Uses AI to identify compounds that target age-related diseases.
  - **Example**: Discovering drugs that repair DNA damage or boost mitochondrial function.

3. Early Detection and Prevention with AI
3.1 AI in Early Diagnosis

- **Wearable Technology**: Devices like Apple Watch and Fitbit use AI to monitor vital signs and detect anomalies.
  - **Use Case**: Identify early markers of cardiovascular disease or diabetes.
- **AI Imaging Tools**: Platforms like Zebra Medical Vision analyze medical imaging to detect conditions like cancer, Alzheimer's, or osteoporosis.

3.2 Predictive Health Models

- **DeepMind Health**: Predicts the onset of acute conditions like kidney failure before symptoms arise.
  - **Use Case**: Enable early interventions to improve outcomes and longevity.

4. Personalized Health and Lifestyle Optimization
4.1 AI for Nutrition

- **Viome**: Analyzes gut microbiomes using AI to recommend personalized diets that promote longevity.
  - **Use Case**: Tailor nutrition to optimize cellular health and reduce inflammation.
- **Nutrigenomics with AI**: Platforms analyze genetic data to design dietary plans.

4.2 AI-Powered Fitness

- **Tonal AI**: Provides personalized strength training recommendations based on user performance.
  - **Use Case**: Maintain muscle mass and bone density with age-appropriate workouts.
- **WHOOP**: Tracks recovery and strain metrics to optimize physical performance and recovery.

4.3 Mental Health and Cognitive Longevity

- **AI for Cognitive Training**: Tools like Lumosity use AI to improve memory, focus, and cognitive flexibility.
  - **Use Case**: Delay cognitive decline and maintain mental acuity.
- **Woebot**: AI-driven mental health chatbot providing therapy and emotional support.

5. AI in Anti-Aging Treatments and Therapies

5.1 Cellular Reprogramming

- AI identifies interventions that reverse cellular aging by reprogramming cells to a younger state.
    - **Example**: Yamanaka factors optimized with AI for regenerative medicine.

5.2 Senescence Targeting

- Senolytics are drugs that target and eliminate senescent (aging) cells.
    - **Tools**: AI predicts which compounds can safely and effectively clear these cells.

5.3 Skin and Aesthetic Longevity

- AI platforms like **SkinAI** analyze skin conditions and recommend anti-aging treatments.
    - **Use Case**: Develop personalized skincare regimens to maintain youthful skin.

6. AI and Environmental Factors for Longevity

6.1 Air Quality Monitoring

- AI systems like **BreezoMeter** analyze environmental data to provide real-time air quality updates.
    - **Use Case**: Reduce exposure to pollutants that accelerate aging.

6.2 Smart Home Technology

- AI-powered smart homes optimize living environments for better sleep, reduced stress, and overall health.
    - **Example**: Smart lighting systems that align with circadian rhythms.

6.3 Climate Change Adaptation

- AI predicts climate-related health risks and suggests adaptive measures.
    - **Use Case**: Prepare communities for extreme weather events that impact longevity.

7. AI in Longevity Economics
7.1 Reducing Healthcare Costs

- AI streamlines diagnostics and treatment, reducing the financial burden of aging-related diseases.
- **Example**: Predictive AI minimizes hospitalizations by addressing issues proactively.

7.2 Longevity Investment Opportunities

- AI-driven startups focused on healthcare and wellness offer lucrative investment options.
    - **Example**: Companies like **Calico** and **AgeX Therapeutics**.

8. Challenges and Ethical Considerations in AI for Longevity
8.1 Equity and Accessibility

- **Challenge**: Ensuring AI-driven longevity technologies are accessible to all, not just the wealthy.
- **Solution**: Develop affordable AI solutions for global health initiatives.

8.2 Data Privacy

- Protect sensitive health data used in AI systems.
- **Example**: Use encryption and comply with GDPR regulations.

8.3 Ethical Boundaries

- Address potential ethical dilemmas, such as the societal impact of significantly extended lifespans.

9. Future Trends in AI and Longevity

- **Digital Twin Technology**: AI creates virtual models of individuals for real-time health monitoring and intervention testing.
- **Bioprinting and AI**: AI optimizes 3D printing of tissues and organs for transplantation.
- **AI-Driven Longevity Clinics**: Facilities offering AI-based diagnostics, therapies, and health optimization programs.

Conclusion: AI as a Catalyst for a Longer, Healthier Life

AI is reshaping the landscape of longevity, offering tools and insights that were once the realm of science fiction. From early detection of diseases to personalized health optimization, AI is unlocking the potential for longer, healthier, and more productive lives.

By embracing AI-driven innovations, individuals and organizations can not only enhance the quality of life but also redefine what it means to age gracefully. The future of longevity is here, and AI is leading the way.

Chapter 24: Combining Human Creativity with AI Intelligence

Introduction: Unlocking New Frontiers with Human-AI Collaboration

Human creativity is boundless, characterized by imagination, emotion, and innovation. Artificial intelligence (AI), on the other hand, excels in data processing, pattern recognition, and speed. The convergence of these two forces creates unparalleled opportunities for solving problems, driving innovation, and pushing the boundaries of what's possible. However, the key to unlocking these opportunities lies in finding the right balance between human ingenuity and AI capabilities.

In this chapter, we explore how humans and AI can work together to amplify creativity, enhance productivity, and create transformative outcomes. By examining practical applications, ethical considerations, and future trends, we will uncover how this symbiotic relationship can shape industries and society.

1. Understanding the Synergy Between Human Creativity and AI

1.1 What Human Creativity Brings to the Table

- **Imagination**: The ability to envision possibilities beyond the current data.
- **Emotion**: Understanding nuance, empathy, and subjective experiences.
- **Intuition**: Making leaps in reasoning that are not data-driven but inspired by experience.

1.2 AI's Strengths in Creative Collaboration

- **Speed and Efficiency**: Processing vast datasets to uncover insights in seconds.
- **Pattern Recognition**: Identifying trends and correlations invisible to the human eye.
- **Iterative Testing**: Rapidly generating and refining ideas based on feedback.

1.3 The Power of Collaboration

- Humans provide the vision and context; AI provides the tools and insights to bring ideas to life.

2. Applications of Human-AI Collaboration

2.1 Art and Design

- **Generative Art**: AI tools like **DALL·E** and **DeepArt** create visual art based on human input.
  - **Use Case**: Artists can use AI to explore new styles and techniques.
- **Architectural Design**: AI platforms like **Spacemaker** optimize building designs for aesthetics and functionality.
  - **Use Case**: Architects balance creativity with data-driven insights for sustainable designs.

2.2 Writing and Storytelling

- **AI-Assisted Writing**: Tools like **Jasper AI** and **Grammarly** help writers generate, refine, and edit content.
  - **Use Case**: Authors use AI to brainstorm plot ideas or create character profiles.
- **Interactive Storytelling**: AI in video games enables dynamic narratives that respond to player actions.
  - **Example**: AI-driven NPCs (non-playable characters) in open-world games.

2.3 Music and Sound

- **AI Music Composition**: Platforms like **AIVA** and **Amper Music** compose original scores based on user input.
  - **Use Case**: Musicians collaborate with AI to experiment with genres and harmonies.
- **Sound Design**: AI analyzes soundscapes to create immersive environments for films and games.

2.4 Business and Marketing

- **AI-Powered Campaigns**: Tools like **AdCreative.ai** generate tailored marketing content.
  - **Use Case**: Marketers combine their audience understanding with AI's data analysis to craft impactful campaigns.
- **Brand Strategy**: AI tools like **Brand24** analyze consumer sentiment to inform creative direction.

3. Enhancing Creativity with AI Tools
3.1 Brainstorming and Ideation

- **MindMeister with AI**: Facilitates brainstorming sessions by organizing ideas visually.
    - **Use Case**: Teams can generate and refine ideas collaboratively.

3.2 Prototyping and Iteration

- **Figma AI**: Enhances UI/UX design by automating repetitive tasks and suggesting design improvements.
    - **Use Case**: Designers iterate faster with AI-generated wireframes and layouts.

3.3 Content Generation

- **Copy.ai**: Automates content creation for blogs, ads, and emails.
    - **Use Case**: Writers save time by focusing on strategy while AI handles drafts.

4. Industries Transformed by Human-AI Collaboration
4.1 Healthcare

- **AI in Diagnostics**: Doctors combine their expertise with AI tools like **PathAI** to detect diseases early.
    - **Use Case**: AI analyzes medical images while doctors interpret results in context.

4.2 Education

- **Adaptive Learning Platforms**: Teachers use tools like **Knewton** to tailor lessons to individual student needs.
    - **Use Case**: AI optimizes teaching strategies while educators provide emotional support.

4.3 Film and Media

- **AI in Scriptwriting**: Tools like **ScriptBook** predict audience reception to movie scripts.
    - **Use Case**: Screenwriters balance creative storytelling with data insights.

5. The Creative Process in the Age of AI

5.1 Co-Creation Models

- Humans and AI engage in a feedback loop where each informs the other.
    - **Example**: A designer sketches a concept, and AI refines it with data-driven suggestions.

5.2 AI as a Muse

- AI can spark new ideas by generating unexpected outputs.
    - **Use Case**: Writers use AI-generated prompts to overcome creative blocks.

5.3 Expanding Possibilities

- AI expands the boundaries of what's possible, enabling creativity that was previously unattainable.
    - **Example**: AI helps fashion designers visualize clothing made from innovative materials.

6. Ethical Considerations in Human-AI Creativity

6.1 Ownership and Attribution

- Who owns the intellectual property of AI-assisted creations?
    - **Solution**: Develop clear guidelines for shared credit and rights.

6.2 Authenticity

- Ensuring that AI doesn't dilute the authenticity of human expression.
    - **Example**: Use AI to complement, not replace, human storytelling.

6.3 Bias in AI Tools

- AI can perpetuate biases present in its training data.
    - **Solution**: Regularly audit AI models to ensure fairness.

7. Challenges of Human-AI Collaboration
7.1 Over-Reliance on AI

- Risk: Creativity becomes homogenized due to overuse of AI-generated templates.
    - **Solution**: Balance AI automation with human originality.

7.2 Loss of Human Skills

- Risk: Over-dependence on AI could lead to atrophy of creative skills.
    - **Solution**: Use AI as a tool to enhance, not replace, skill development.

8. Future Trends in Human-AI Collaboration
8.1 AI-Powered Virtual Collaborators

- **Example**: AI-powered avatars that work alongside humans in creative fields.

8.2 Immersive Experiences

- AI and augmented reality (AR) creating interactive art installations and experiences.

8.3 Decentralized Creative Platforms

- Blockchain-integrated AI platforms ensuring transparent collaboration and revenue sharing.

Conclusion: The Future of Creativity is Collaborative

Human creativity and AI intelligence are not competitors; they are collaborators in shaping the future. By combining human intuition, emotion, and originality with AI's analytical prowess and efficiency, we can unlock opportunities that were once beyond imagination.

The balance lies in leveraging AI to enhance and expand human potential without losing the essence of what makes creativity uniquely human. The strategies and insights in this chapter empower individuals and industries to embrace this collaboration and redefine the boundaries of innovation. The future of creativity is here, and it's powered by the synergy of human and machine.

Chapter 25: Your AI Trillionaire Journey

Introduction: A Vision for Your AI-Driven Legacy

The age of artificial intelligence (AI) is here, offering unprecedented opportunities for wealth creation, innovation, and impact. Becoming an AI trillionaire is not just about accumulating financial success—it's about leveraging AI to build a lasting legacy that transforms industries, uplifts communities, and redefines the future. This journey requires vision, strategy, and an unrelenting commitment to integrating AI into every aspect of your life and business.

This final chapter brings together all the elements discussed in this book, offering a comprehensive roadmap to guide you in building your AI-driven legacy. From identifying opportunities to overcoming challenges, we'll cover how to leverage AI tools, foster innovation, and ensure your efforts create meaningful and lasting impact.

1. Crafting Your Vision: The Foundation of Legacy

1.1 Defining Your Purpose

- **Ask Yourself**:
    - What do you want to achieve with AI-driven wealth?
    - How do you want to be remembered in your industry, community, or the world?

1.2 Setting Long-Term Goals

- Combine financial milestones with transformative initiatives:
    - Example: Use AI-generated wealth to fund groundbreaking research or solve global challenges like poverty, education, or climate change.

1.3 Aligning AI with Your Vision

- Identify how AI tools can amplify your efforts in achieving your goals.
    - Example: AI for predictive analysis in investments, automation in business operations, or scaling education programs.

2. Strategies for Sustainable Wealth Creation with AI
2.1 Diversify AI Investments

- Invest across industries poised for disruption, including:
    - **Healthcare**: AI-driven drug discovery and personalized medicine.
    - **Finance**: Algorithmic trading and fraud detection.
    - **Education**: AI-powered adaptive learning platforms.
    - **Energy**: AI for renewable energy optimization.

2.2 Build AI-Driven Businesses

- Create businesses that integrate AI to solve real-world problems:
    - Example: Develop an AI-powered platform for sustainable farming.

2.3 Focus on Emerging Markets

- Leverage AI to tap into underserved markets:
    - Example: Use AI tools for microfinance in developing regions.

3. Building Your Personal Brand as an AI Leader
3.1 Establish Thought Leadership

- Share your vision and insights through:
    - Public speaking.
    - Publishing books, articles, or blogs on AI innovation.
    - Engaging with global audiences via social media platforms.

3.2 Create a Network of AI Innovators

- Surround yourself with like-minded individuals who are pioneers in AI.
    - Join AI-focused organizations and communities.
    - Invest in or mentor AI-driven startups.

3.3 Use AI to Amplify Your Reach

- Leverage AI tools for personal branding:
    - Example: AI-powered content creation for social media and public relations.

4. Embracing Innovation and Continuous Learning
4.1 Stay Ahead of Trends

- Regularly analyze emerging AI trends and adapt your strategies:
  - Monitor advancements in areas like quantum computing, decentralized AI, and digital twin technologies.

4.2 Commit to Lifelong Learning

- Use AI-driven learning platforms like **Coursera** or **LinkedIn Learning** to stay updated on AI advancements and business strategies.

4.3 Encourage Experimentation

- Foster a culture of innovation by experimenting with new AI tools and approaches:
  - Example: Pilot AI-powered projects in sustainability, healthcare, or education.

5. Overcoming Challenges on Your AI Journey
5.1 Addressing Ethical Concerns

- Develop clear ethical guidelines for your AI applications:
  - Focus on transparency, fairness, and inclusivity in AI systems.

5.2 Managing Risks

- Mitigate risks associated with AI adoption:
  - Example: Use robust cybersecurity measures to protect AI systems and data.

5.3 Balancing Automation and Human Input

- Ensure that AI enhances, rather than replaces, human capabilities.

6. Creating a Global Impact with AI
6.1 Social Responsibility Initiatives

- Use AI-generated wealth to fund initiatives that address global challenges:
    - Example: AI for disaster prediction and response in vulnerable regions.

6.2 Environmental Sustainability

- Invest in AI-powered solutions for renewable energy, carbon capture, and sustainable agriculture.

6.3 Empowering Communities

- Develop AI-driven platforms to improve education, healthcare, and financial inclusion in underserved areas.

7. Building a Legacy of Innovation and Impact
7.1 Documenting Your Journey

- Share your story through books, documentaries, or public appearances to inspire future generations.

7.2 Mentoring the Next Generation

- Invest time and resources in mentoring young innovators in AI.
    - Example: Sponsor scholarships for AI education.

7.3 Creating Enduring Systems

- Establish foundations or organizations that continue your work:
    - Example: A foundation that funds AI research or sustainability projects.

8. Leveraging AI to Achieve Work-Life Harmony
8.1 Automating Routine Tasks

- Use AI to manage daily tasks, freeing time for strategic thinking and personal pursuits.

8.2 Enhancing Well-Being

- Incorporate AI tools for mental and physical health optimization:
    - Example: AI-driven fitness trackers or meditation apps.

8.3 Finding Fulfillment

- Balance wealth generation with meaningful activities that align with your values.

9. Future-Proofing Your Legacy with AI
9.1 Anticipating Disruptions

- Stay adaptable by monitoring emerging technologies that complement or challenge AI.

9.2 Investing in Resilience

- Build systems and organizations that can evolve with technological advancements.

9.3 Ensuring Ethical AI Practices

- Commit to responsible AI development and implementation to build trust and credibility.

Conclusion: Your AI Trillionaire Legacy Awaits

The journey to becoming an AI trillionaire is not just about wealth—it's about creating a lasting impact that transcends generations. By combining innovation, vision, and strategic action, you can leverage AI to build a legacy that transforms industries, uplifts communities, and redefines what's possible.

The strategies outlined in this chapter empower you to integrate AI into every aspect of your journey, ensuring a future of success, influence, and purpose. Your legacy as an AI trillionaire begins today—embrace the opportunities, overcome the challenges, and shape the future with the transformative power of AI.

Appendix A: Essential AI Tools

Comprehensive List of AI Software and Platforms for Every Industry

AI tools have revolutionized the way we approach tasks across industries, enabling efficiency, innovation, and unparalleled scalability. This appendix provides a detailed list of essential AI tools, categorized by their applications, to help you harness AI in every area of your personal and professional endeavors.

1. AI Tools for Business and Productivity

1.1 Automation and Workflow Management

- **Zapier**: Connects applications to automate repetitive tasks.
    - **Use Case**: Automatically transfer data between apps like Gmail, Slack, and Google Sheets.
- **IFTTT (If This Then That)**: Simplifies automation across devices and platforms.
    - **Use Case**: Automate daily workflows like syncing calendars and reminders.

1.2 Virtual Assistants

- **Google Assistant**: Offers hands-free scheduling, reminders, and quick answers.
    - **Use Case**: Automate personal and work-related tasks.
- **Microsoft Cortana**: Manages reminders and integrates with Microsoft Office tools.

1.3 Project Management

- **Asana AI**: Uses AI insights to recommend task prioritization and streamline workflows.
- **Monday.com**: AI-enhanced project management with customizable workflows.

2. AI Tools for Marketing and Advertising

2.1 Content Creation

- **Jasper AI**: Generates high-quality marketing copy, blogs, and social media content.
    - **Use Case**: Create compelling marketing campaigns effortlessly.
- **Copy.ai**: Automates writing tasks, from headlines to ad copy.

2.2 SEO Optimization

- **Ahrefs AI**: Conducts keyword research and competitive analysis.
- **Surfer SEO**: Optimizes content for search engine visibility.

2.3 Analytics and Campaign Management

- **Hootsuite Insights**: Monitors and analyzes social media campaigns.
- **HubSpot AI**: Automates customer engagement and email marketing.

3. AI Tools for Finance and Investing

3.1 Financial Management

- **QuickBooks AI**: Automates accounting, invoicing, and expense tracking.
- **YNAB (You Need A Budget)**: AI-driven budgeting tool for personal and business finances.

3.2 Stock Market Analysis

- **Kavout**: Uses predictive algorithms to identify high-potential stocks.
- **QuantConnect**: Provides AI-driven backtesting and trading strategies.

3.3 Cryptocurrency

- **Coinrule**: AI-based crypto trading automation platform.
- **Pionex**: Offers built-in AI trading bots for cryptocurrency.

4. AI Tools for Education
4.1 Personalized Learning

- **Khan Academy AI**: Delivers tailored lessons based on student performance.
- **Duolingo AI**: Adapts language lessons to individual learning speeds.

4.2 Skill Development

- **Coursera AI**: Recommends courses to help learners achieve their career goals.
- **EdApp**: Provides bite-sized, AI-powered microlearning content.

4.3 Educational Content Creation

- **Canva AI**: Creates visually appealing presentations and learning materials.
- **Prezi AI**: Enhances interactive learning through dynamic presentations.

5. AI Tools for Healthcare
5.1 Diagnostics

- **Zebra Medical Vision**: Analyzes medical imaging to detect conditions like cancer and osteoporosis.
- **PathAI**: Enhances diagnostic accuracy by analyzing pathology data.

5.2 Telemedicine

- **Babylon Health**: AI-powered health consultation and diagnostic app.
- **Ada Health**: Provides symptom checks and preliminary diagnoses.

5.3 Drug Discovery

- **Insilico Medicine**: Uses AI to identify compounds for drug development.

6. AI Tools for Retail and E-commerce

6.1 Product Recommendations

- **Dynamic Yield**: Personalizes customer shopping experiences with AI.
- **Salesforce Einstein**: Delivers AI-driven recommendations for e-commerce platforms.

6.2 Inventory and Supply Chain Management

- **Blue Yonder**: Optimizes inventory and supply chain operations.
- **ClearMetal**: Uses predictive AI to enhance supply chain visibility.

6.3 Visual Search

- **Syte**: Enables AI-powered visual search for e-commerce sites.

7. AI Tools for Creativity and Media

7.1 Art and Design

- **DALL·E**: Creates unique visuals based on text descriptions.
- **Runway ML**: Offers tools for AI-generated art and video editing.

7.2 Writing

- **Grammarly**: AI-driven tool for improving grammar and writing clarity.
- **Writesonic**: Generates creative writing, including blogs, ads, and stories.

7.3 Music and Sound

- **AIVA**: Composes original music for various applications.
- **Amper Music**: Creates royalty-free background scores.

8. AI Tools for Transportation and Logistics

8.1 Route Optimization

- **Onfleet AI**: Optimizes delivery routes for logistics companies.
- **Google Maps AI**: Enhances route planning with real-time traffic data.

8.2 Autonomous Vehicles

- **Waymo**: Develops self-driving technology for autonomous cars.
- **Tesla AI**: Powers autopilot features in Tesla vehicles.

8.3 Fleet Management

- **Fleetio**: AI-powered fleet tracking and maintenance planning.

9. AI Tools for Cybersecurity

9.1 Threat Detection

- **Darktrace**: Uses AI to detect and mitigate cyber threats.
- **CrowdStrike**: Provides real-time threat intelligence.

9.2 Data Protection

- **IBM QRadar**: Identifies vulnerabilities and ensures compliance.

9.3 Fraud Prevention

- **FICO Falcon**: Detects fraudulent transactions in financial systems.

10. AI Tools for Environmental Sustainability

10.1 Climate Change

- **Pachama**: Monitors and validates forest conservation projects.
- **DeepMind Energy**: Optimizes energy grids to reduce carbon footprints.

10.2 Agriculture

- **FarmLogs**: Uses AI to monitor crop health and predict yields.
- **Taranis**: Provides AI-powered aerial imagery for precision agriculture.

10.3 Waste Management

- **Recycleye**: AI-powered sorting system for waste management.

Conclusion: Your Toolbox for an AI-Driven Future

This comprehensive list highlights the diversity of AI tools available for various industries. By leveraging these platforms, you can optimize workflows, enhance creativity, improve decision-making, and unlock new opportunities in your journey toward AI-driven success. Keep exploring and experimenting with these tools to ensure that you stay at the forefront of innovation.

Appendix B: Trillionaire Case Studies

Real-Life Examples of Individuals and Companies Leveraging AI for Wealth

The transformative power of artificial intelligence (AI) is evident in the success stories of visionary individuals and companies who have leveraged it to create significant wealth. This appendix provides an in-depth look at case studies that showcase how AI has been used to disrupt industries, build empires, and pave the way for unprecedented financial success.

1. Elon Musk and Tesla

1.1 Overview

Elon Musk, the founder of Tesla, has revolutionized the automotive and energy industries using AI. Tesla's AI-driven innovations have not only made electric vehicles mainstream but also redefined autonomous driving technology.

1.2 Key AI Strategies

- **Autonomous Driving**: Tesla's **Full Self-Driving (FSD)** feature uses neural networks to navigate complex road conditions.
- **AI in Manufacturing**: Tesla employs AI-powered robotics and predictive analytics to optimize production processes.
- **Energy Management**: Tesla's AI-driven energy solutions, such as Powerwall and Megapack, enhance energy storage and distribution.

1.3 Financial Impact

- Tesla's valuation exceeded $1 trillion in 2021, fueled by its leadership in AI and renewable energy.

2. Sundar Pichai and Google

2.1 Overview

Under Sundar Pichai's leadership, Google has leveraged AI across its platforms to dominate the tech industry and create wealth through innovation and efficiency.

2.2 Key AI Strategies

- **Search and Advertising**: Google's AI algorithms power its search engine and **Google Ads**, providing highly targeted advertising capabilities.
- **AI Cloud Services: Google Cloud AI** offers enterprise solutions, including machine learning and data analytics.
- **AI in Products**: Innovations like **Google Assistant**, **Google Translate**, and **DeepMind** have revolutionized user experiences.

2.3 Financial Impact

- Alphabet Inc., Google's parent company, surpassed a $2 trillion valuation, driven by AI's integration into its core services and products.

3. Jeff Bezos and Amazon

3.1 Overview

Amazon, under Jeff Bezos, has utilized AI to dominate e-commerce, logistics, and cloud computing, creating a financial juggernaut.

3.2 Key AI Strategies

- **Recommendation Engines**: Amazon's AI-driven recommendation system significantly boosts sales by personalizing customer experiences.
- **Supply Chain and Logistics**: AI optimizes inventory management, route planning, and delivery efficiency.
- **Cloud Computing**: **Amazon Web Services (AWS)** provides AI and machine learning solutions to businesses worldwide.

3.3 Financial Impact

- Amazon's valuation crossed $1.7 trillion, with AI playing a pivotal role in its scalability and efficiency.

4. Jensen Huang and NVIDIA

4.1 Overview

Jensen Huang, co-founder of NVIDIA, has positioned the company as a leader in AI hardware and software, driving exponential growth.

4.2 Key AI Strategies

- **AI Hardware**: NVIDIA's **GPUs** (graphics processing units) are essential for AI development and deployment, powering everything from autonomous vehicles to AI research.
- **AI Software**: Platforms like **NVIDIA AI Enterprise** provide end-to-end AI solutions for businesses.
- **AI in Gaming and Media**: NVIDIA's real-time rendering and AI-powered enhancements have transformed the gaming and entertainment industries.

4.3 Financial Impact

- NVIDIA reached a market capitalization of over $1 trillion in 2023, largely due to its dominance in AI technology.

5. OpenAI: Democratizing AI Wealth Creation

5.1 Overview

Founded by Sam Altman and Elon Musk, OpenAI has been at the forefront of AI innovation, creating tools like ChatGPT and DALL·E that empower individuals and businesses.

5.2 Key AI Strategies

- **Natural Language Processing (NLP)**: Tools like ChatGPT revolutionize how businesses and individuals interact with AI for tasks like content creation and customer support.
- **Generative AI**: DALL·E enables the creation of visual content, opening new avenues in art and design.
- **AI Research**: OpenAI continually advances AI's capabilities, pushing the boundaries of machine learning.

5.3 Financial Impact

- OpenAI's commercial success has been fueled by partnerships with tech giants like Microsoft and widespread adoption of its tools.

6. Alibaba: AI in E-Commerce and Beyond

6.1 Overview

Alibaba, founded by Jack Ma, has integrated AI across its platforms to dominate e-commerce, logistics, and cloud computing in Asia.

6.2 Key AI Strategies

- **AI in E-Commerce**: Alibaba's recommendation algorithms and chatbots enhance the shopping experience.
- **Logistics Optimization**: AI-powered warehouses and delivery systems ensure efficiency.
- **AI in Finance**: Alibaba's financial arm, Ant Group, uses AI for credit scoring and fraud detection.

6.3 Financial Impact

- Alibaba's valuation soared to over $700 billion, with AI as a driving force behind its success.

7. IBM: Revolutionizing Business Solutions with AI

7.1 Overview

IBM has been a pioneer in AI through its **Watson** platform, providing AI-driven solutions to industries ranging from healthcare to finance.

7.2 Key AI Strategies

- **AI in Healthcare**: Watson assists in diagnosing diseases and personalizing treatments.
- **Business Analytics**: AI-driven tools like **IBM Planning Analytics** optimize business operations.
- **Cybersecurity**: AI-powered tools enhance threat detection and prevention.

7.3 Financial Impact

- IBM remains a leader in AI for enterprise solutions, significantly contributing to its $100 billion valuation.

8. Baidu: Leading AI Innovations in China

8.1 Overview

Baidu, often referred to as the "Google of China," has heavily invested in AI to lead advancements in autonomous driving and natural language processing.

8.2 Key AI Strategies

- **Apollo Autonomous Driving**: Baidu's self-driving car platform leverages AI for navigation and safety.
- **AI-Powered Search**: AI enhances search capabilities and user experience.
- **AI Cloud**: Baidu's cloud computing services integrate AI for enterprise clients.

8.3 Financial Impact

- Baidu's success in AI innovation has driven its market value to over $50 billion.

9. Palantir: AI for Big Data and Security

9.1 Overview

Palantir, founded by Alex Karp, specializes in AI-driven big data analytics for governments and corporations.

9.2 Key AI Strategies

- **AI in National Security**: Analyzes large datasets to detect threats and enable decision-making.
- **Predictive Analytics**: Assists businesses in forecasting trends and mitigating risks.

9.3 Financial Impact

- Palantir's valuation has grown to over $40 billion, fueled by its proprietary AI solutions.

10. Stripe: AI in Fintech

10.1 Overview

Stripe, co-founded by Patrick and John Collison, leverages AI to revolutionize online payments and financial services.

10.2 Key AI Strategies

- **Fraud Detection**: AI identifies and prevents fraudulent transactions.
- **Payment Optimization**: Machine learning enhances payment success rates.

10.3 Financial Impact

- Stripe's valuation exceeds $95 billion, making it one of the most valuable fintech companies globally.

Conclusion: Learning from AI Titans

The success stories of individuals and companies leveraging AI provide a blueprint for creating wealth and driving innovation. By understanding their strategies, tools, and approaches, you can adopt similar methodologies to chart your path toward success. These case studies highlight that AI is not just a tool—it's a transformative force that, when harnessed effectively, can redefine industries and create legacies.

The question isn't whether you can become an AI-driven success story; the question is: when will you start?

Appendix C: AI Wealth Strategies Checklist

Step-by-Step Guide to Implementing the Concepts in the Book

This appendix provides a comprehensive, actionable checklist to help you implement the AI-driven wealth strategies discussed in this book. By following these steps, you can effectively leverage AI tools, identify opportunities, and create sustainable wealth while positioning yourself for long-term success.

Step 1: Define Your AI Wealth Vision

1. **Identify Your Goals**:
   - What do you want to achieve with AI-driven wealth?
   - How does your vision align with personal, financial, and societal impact?
2. **Select a Focus Area**:
   - Choose an industry or niche that aligns with your skills, interests, and AI capabilities (e.g., healthcare, finance, retail, education).
3. **Establish Metrics for Success**:
   - Define measurable outcomes such as revenue targets, project milestones, or audience growth.

Step 2: Build Your AI Knowledge Base

1. **Understand AI Fundamentals**:
   - Learn key concepts like machine learning, neural networks, and data analysis.
2. **Explore AI Applications in Your Industry**:
   - Research case studies and AI tools relevant to your chosen field.
3. **Commit to Lifelong Learning**:
   - Use platforms like **Coursera**, **LinkedIn Learning**, and **Khan Academy AI** to stay updated on AI advancements.

Step 3: Select and Master AI Tools

1. **Automation Tools**:
   - Use platforms like **Zapier** and **IFTTT** to streamline workflows.
2. **Data Analysis Tools**:
   - Adopt tools like **Tableau**, **Power BI**, or **Google Analytics** for insights into trends and patterns.
3. **Industry-Specific Tools**:
   - Choose AI software tailored to your industry, such as **DeepMind** for healthcare or **Dynamic Yield** for e-commerce.
4. **Content Creation Tools**:
   - Enhance your productivity with tools like **Jasper AI** (writing), **DALL·E** (visuals), and **Canva AI** (design).

Step 4: Develop AI-Driven Business Models

1. **Identify Problems to Solve**:
    - Pinpoint inefficiencies, gaps, or challenges in your industry where AI can provide solutions.
2. **Design Scalable Solutions**:
    - Leverage AI to create products or services that can scale rapidly.
3. **Test and Iterate**:
    - Use AI tools to simulate outcomes, gather feedback, and refine your approach.
4. **Automate Processes**:
    - Implement AI-driven automation in areas like customer support (chatbots), marketing (AI analytics), and operations (predictive maintenance).

Step 5: Leverage AI for Marketing and Branding

1. **Build a Personal Brand**:
    - Use AI tools like **Grammarly**, **Hootsuite Insights**, and **AdCreative.ai** to craft compelling content and campaigns.
2. **Engage Your Audience**:
    - Automate personalized interactions through chatbots like **ManyChat** and CRM platforms like **HubSpot AI**.
3. **Optimize Campaigns**:
    - Analyze marketing performance with tools like **Google Ads AI** and **Facebook Ads Manager AI**.

Step 6: Invest in AI-Powered Opportunities

1. **Diversify Investments**:
    - Allocate resources across AI-driven industries like healthcare, fintech, and renewable energy.
2. **Explore AI Startups**:
    - Invest in innovative startups that leverage AI for disruptive solutions.
3. **Adopt AI-Enhanced Trading**:
    - Use platforms like **Kavout** or **QuantConnect** for algorithmic trading and market predictions.

Step 7: Enhance Productivity with AI

1. **Time Management Tools**:
    - Use **Clockwise** and **RescueTime** to optimize your schedule and eliminate inefficiencies.
2. **Task Automation**:
    - Streamline repetitive tasks with tools like **Monday.com AI** and **Asana AI**.
3. **Focus Tools**:
    - Leverage apps like **Focus@Will** and **Serene** to maintain concentration during critical work.

Step 8: Foster Innovation Through Human-AI Collaboration

1. **Co-Creation**:
    - Partner with AI to generate ideas and refine creative outputs (e.g., **DALL·E** for visuals, **AIVA** for music).
2. **Experimentation**:
    - Use AI simulations to test new business models or products.
3. **Empower Teams with AI**:
    - Train employees to use AI tools, enabling innovation at every level of your organization.

Step 9: Monitor and Adapt to Emerging Trends

1. **Track AI Advancements**:
    - Stay informed about breakthroughs in AI research and applications.
2. **Analyze Competitors**:
    - Use tools like **Brandwatch** to monitor competitors' AI strategies and adjust your approach accordingly.
3. **Adopt Emerging Technologies**:
    - Explore trends like quantum computing, decentralized AI, and digital twins to stay ahead of the curve.

Step 10: Scale Impact and Build Your Legacy

1. **Focus on Sustainability**:
    - Invest in AI-driven solutions for environmental and social impact, such as **Pachama** (reforestation) or **DeepMind Energy** (renewables).
2. **Mentor the Next Generation**:
    - Share your knowledge and experiences to inspire and guide future innovators.
3. **Document Your Journey**:
    - Write books, give talks, or create content to showcase your contributions and inspire others.
4. **Establish Enduring Systems**:
    - Create foundations or organizations that continue your work, ensuring a lasting legacy.

Step 11: Overcome Challenges and Risks

1. **Mitigate Bias in AI**:
    - Regularly audit AI models to ensure fairness and inclusivity.
2. **Address Privacy Concerns**:
    - Comply with regulations like GDPR and CCPA to protect user data.
3. **Balance Automation with Human Oversight**:
    - Ensure AI systems complement human intuition and creativity.

Step 12: Evaluate and Refine Your Strategies

1. **Track Progress**:
    - Use dashboards like **Tableau** or **Power BI** to measure your financial and impact metrics.
2. **Gather Feedback**:
    - Continuously seek input from customers, employees, and stakeholders.
3. **Adapt to Changes**:
    - Remain flexible and willing to pivot as market conditions and technologies evolve.

Conclusion: Your AI Wealth Journey Awaits

This checklist is your roadmap to transforming AI-driven opportunities into lasting wealth and impact. By following these steps, you can integrate AI into every facet of your personal and professional life, ensuring a legacy of innovation, success, and global influence.

Start your journey today—every step brings you closer to becoming an AI-powered visionary who shapes the future.

Appendix D: Future-Proof Investments

Key Industries and Technologies to Watch in the AI Era

As artificial intelligence (AI) continues to revolutionize industries, identifying future-proof investments becomes critical for sustained financial growth and relevance. This appendix provides a detailed guide to key industries and technologies poised for massive growth, highlighting opportunities to capitalize on the AI-driven economy.

1. The Healthcare Revolution

1.1 Precision Medicine

- **What It Is**: Personalized treatment plans based on genetic, lifestyle, and environmental factors.
- **Key Technologies**: AI-driven genetic analysis tools like CRISPR, AI-enabled diagnostics, and wearable health monitors.
- **Why It's Future-Proof**: The demand for tailored healthcare solutions is growing as populations age.
- **Investment Opportunities**: Companies like **Deep Genomics**, **23andMe**, and **Illumina**.

1.2 Telemedicine and Remote Diagnostics

- **What It Is**: Virtual healthcare consultations and AI-powered diagnostic tools.
- **Key Technologies**: Platforms like **Babylon Health** and **Teladoc Health**.
- **Why It's Future-Proof**: Increased adoption due to accessibility and cost-effectiveness.

1.3 Drug Discovery

- **What It Is**: AI algorithms accelerating the discovery of new drugs and therapies.
- **Key Technologies**: AI platforms like **Insilico Medicine** and **Atomwise**.
- **Why It's Future-Proof**: Shortens time-to-market for life-saving treatments.

2. Financial Technology (FinTech)
2.1 AI-Powered Trading

- **What It Is**: Algorithms analyzing market trends for real-time investment decisions.
- **Key Technologies**: Platforms like **Kavout** and **Numerai**.
- **Why It's Future-Proof**: AI outperforms human traders in speed and accuracy.

2.2 Decentralized Finance (DeFi)

- **What It Is**: Blockchain-powered financial services without intermediaries.
- **Key Technologies**: AI-enhanced DeFi platforms like **Aave** and **Compound**.
- **Why It's Future-Proof**: Disrupts traditional banking and democratizes financial access.

2.3 Fraud Detection and Cybersecurity

- **What It Is**: AI tools that identify and prevent fraudulent activities.
- **Key Technologies**: Companies like **Darktrace**, **CrowdStrike**, and **Zest AI**.
- **Why It's Future-Proof**: Cyber threats are evolving, increasing demand for AI-driven security solutions.

3. Energy and Sustainability
3.1 Renewable Energy Optimization

- **What It Is**: AI managing renewable energy grids for efficiency and reliability.
- **Key Technologies**: Platforms like **Google DeepMind Energy** and **Grid Edge**.
- **Why It's Future-Proof**: Governments and industries are prioritizing clean energy transitions.

3.2 Carbon Capture and Climate Tech

- **What It Is**: AI systems predicting and mitigating environmental impact.
- **Key Technologies**: **Pachama** (reforestation analytics) and **Climeworks** (carbon capture).
- **Why It's Future-Proof**: The global push toward net-zero emissions creates a growing market.

3.3 Smart Grids and Energy Storage

- **What It Is**: AI optimizing energy distribution and battery storage systems.
- **Key Technologies**: Tesla's **Powerwall**, **Siemens Smart Grid**, and **NextEra Energy AI**.
- **Why It's Future-Proof**: Increasing reliance on renewable energy necessitates advanced grid solutions.

4. Autonomous Transportation
4.1 Self-Driving Vehicles

- **What It Is**: AI-powered autonomous cars, trucks, and delivery systems.
- **Key Technologies**: Companies like **Waymo**, **Cruise**, and **Tesla**.
- **Why It's Future-Proof**: The logistics and transport sectors are shifting toward automation.

4.2 Drones and Aerial Mobility

- **What It Is**: AI-enabled drones for delivery, surveillance, and emergency response.
- **Key Technologies**: Platforms like **Skydio** and **Zipline**.
- **Why It's Future-Proof**: Expanding use cases across industries like e-commerce, healthcare, and defense.

5. Artificial Intelligence and Automation
5.1 AI Software Development

- **What It Is**: Tools and platforms advancing machine learning and AI applications.
- **Key Technologies**: **OpenAI**, **Hugging Face**, and **DataRobot**.
- **Why It's Future-Proof**: Demand for AI solutions spans all industries.

5.2 Robotic Process Automation (RPA)

- **What It Is**: Software robots automating repetitive business tasks.
- **Key Technologies**: **UiPath**, **Automation Anywhere**, and **Blue Prism**.
- **Why It's Future-Proof**: Companies are increasingly looking to reduce costs and improve efficiency.

5.3 AI in Creative Fields

- **What It Is**: Tools generating art, music, and content.
- **Key Technologies**: **DALL·E**, **AIVA**, and **Runway ML**.
- **Why It's Future-Proof**: Creative industries are embracing AI for enhanced productivity and innovation.

6. E-commerce and Retail
6.1 Personalization Engines

- **What It Is**: AI tools delivering tailored shopping experiences.
- **Key Technologies: Dynamic Yield, Salesforce Einstein**, and **Nosto**.
- **Why It's Future-Proof**: Personalization drives customer loyalty and higher conversion rates.

6.2 Supply Chain and Logistics

- **What It Is**: AI optimizing inventory management, delivery routes, and demand forecasting.
- **Key Technologies: Blue Yonder** and **ClearMetal**.
- **Why It's Future-Proof**: Efficiency and cost savings are critical for e-commerce scalability.

6.3 Augmented Reality (AR) Shopping

- **What It Is**: AI-powered AR platforms allowing virtual product trials.
- **Key Technologies: Syte** and **Threekit**.
- **Why It's Future-Proof**: Enhances customer engagement and reduces return rates.

7. Education and Skill Development
7.1 Personalized Learning Platforms

- **What It Is**: AI tailoring lessons to individual learning styles and paces.
- **Key Technologies: Khan Academy AI, Coursera**, and **EdTech AI** startups.
- **Why It's Future-Proof**: Lifelong learning is essential in an evolving job market.

7.2 Corporate Training

- **What It Is**: AI platforms delivering skills training and performance analytics.
- **Key Technologies: Degreed, Udemy for Business**, and **Skillsoft**.
- **Why It's Future-Proof**: Companies need to upskill employees to adapt to technological advancements.

8. Cybersecurity
8.1 AI for Threat Detection

- **What It Is**: AI identifying and neutralizing cyber threats in real-time.
- **Key Technologies: Darktrace, Palo Alto Networks**, and **SentinelOne**.
- **Why It's Future-Proof**: The rise in cybercrime necessitates robust security solutions.

8.2 AI-Driven Privacy Tools

- **What It Is**: Platforms ensuring compliance with data protection regulations.
- **Key Technologies: BigID** and **IBM Security Guardium**.
- **Why It's Future-Proof**: Data privacy is increasingly critical for businesses and governments.

9. Entertainment and Media
9.1 Streaming and Content Recommendation

- **What It Is**: AI curating personalized content recommendations.
- **Key Technologies: Netflix AI, Spotify**, and **YouTube**.
- **Why It's Future-Proof**: Personalization improves user retention and engagement.

9.2 Virtual Production

- **What It Is**: AI-driven tools for film and media production.
- **Key Technologies: Unreal Engine** and **Runway ML**.
- **Why It's Future-Proof**: Reduces costs and expands creative possibilities.

10. Space Exploration
10.1 AI in Space Missions

- **What It Is**: AI supporting mission planning, spacecraft navigation, and data analysis.
- **Key Technologies**: NASA's AI initiatives, **SpaceX**, and **Blue Origin**.
- **Why It's Future-Proof**: The space economy is expanding rapidly, with AI enabling efficiency and innovation.

Conclusion: A Roadmap to Future-Proof Investments

By focusing on these industries and technologies, you position yourself at the forefront of the AI-driven economy. Whether through direct investments, business development, or skill acquisition, these future-proof opportunities ensure long-term growth and relevance in an ever-changing world.

Your journey to leveraging AI for wealth and impact begins with informed, strategic investments in the technologies shaping the future.

Message from the Author:

I hope you enjoyed this book, I love astrology and knew there was not a book such as this out on the shelf. I love metaphysical items as well. Please check out my other books:

-Life of Government Benefits
-My life of Hell
-My life with Hydrocephalus
-Red Sky
-World Domination:Woman's rule
-World Domination:Woman's Rule 2: The War
-Life and Banishment of Apophis: book 1
-The Kidney Friendly Diet
-The Ultimate Hemp Cookbook
-Creating a Dispensary(legally)
-Cleanliness throughout life: the importance of showering from childhood to adulthood.
-Strong Roots: The Risks of Overcoddling children
-Hemp Horoscopes: Cosmic Insights and Earthly Healing
- Celestial Hemp Navigating the Zodiac: Through the Green Cosmos
-Astrological Hemp: Aligning The Stars with Earth's Ancient Herb
-The Astrological Guide to Hemp: Stars, Signs, and Sacred Leaves
-Green Growth: Innovative Marketing Strategies for your Hemp Products and Dispensary
-Cosmic Cannabis
-Astrological Munchies
-Henry The Hemp
-Zodiacal Roots: The Astrological Soul Of Hemp
- **Green Constellations: Intersection of Hemp and Zodiac**
-Hemp in The Houses: An astrological Adventure Through The Cannabis Galaxy
-Galactic Ganja Guide
Heavenly Hemp
Zodiac Leaves
Doctor Who Astrology
Cannastrology
Stellar Satvias and Cosmic Indicas
Celestial Cannabis: A Zodiac Journey
AstroHerbology: The Sky and The Soil: Volume 1
AstroHerbology:Celestial Cannabis:Volume 2
Cosmic Cannabis Cultivation
The Starry Guide to Herbal Harmony: Volume 1
The Starry Guide to Herbal Harmony: Cannabis Universe: Volume 2
Yugioh Astrology: Astrological Guide to Deck, Duels and more
Nightmare Mansion: Echoes of The Abyss

Nightmare Mansion 2: Legacy of Shadows
Nightmare Mansion 3: Shadows of the Forgotten
Nightmare Mansion 4: Echoes of the Damned
The Life and Banishment of Apophis: Book 2
Nightmare Mansion: Halls of Despair
Healing with Herb: Cannabis and Hydrocephalus
Planetary Pot: Aligning with Astrological Herbs: Volume 1
Fast Track to Freedom: 30 Days to Financial Independence Using AI, Assets, and Agile Hustles
Cosmic Hemp Pathways
How to Become Financially Free in 30 Days: 10,000 Paths to Prosperity
Zodiacal Herbage: Astrological Insights: Volume 1
Nightmare Mansion: Whispers in the Walls
The Daleks Invade Atlantis
Henry the hemp and Hydrocephalus

10X The Kidney Friendly Diet
Cannabis Universe: Adult coloring book
Hemp Astrology: The Healing Power of the Stars
Zodiacal Herbage: Astrological Insights: Cannabis Universe: Volume 2
Planetary Pot: Aligning with Astrological Herbs: Cannabis Universes: Volume 2
Doctor Who Meets the Replicators and SG-1: The Ultimate Battle for Survival
Nightmare Mansion: Curse of the Blood Moon
The Celestial Stoner: A Guide to the Zodiac
Cosmic Pleasures: Sex Toy Astrology for Every Sign
Hydrocephalus Astrology: Navigating the Stars and Healing Waters
Lapis and the Mischievous Chocolate Bar

Celestial Positions: Sexual Astrology for Every Sign
Apophis's Shadow Work Journal: **:** A Journey of Self-Discovery and Healing
Kinky Cosmos: Sexual Kink Astrology for Every Sign
Digital Cosmos: The Astrological Digimon Compendium
Stellar Seeds: The Cosmic Guide to Growing with Astrology
Apophis's Daily Gratitude Journal

Cat Astrology: Feline Mysteries of the Cosmos
The Cosmic Kama Sutra: An Astrological Guide to Sexual Positions
Unleash Your Potential: A Guided Journal Powered by AI Insights
Whispers of the Enchanted Grove

Cosmic Pleasures: An Astrological Guide to Sexual Kinks
369, 12 Manifestation Journal
Whisper of the nocturne journal(blank journal for writing or drawing)
The Boogey Book
Locked In Reflection: A Chastity Journey Through Locktober
Generating Wealth Quickly:
How to Generate $100,000 in 24 Hours
Star Magic: Harness the Power of the Universe
The Flatulence Chronicles: A Fart Journal for Self-Discovery
The Doctor and The Death Moth
Seize the Day: A Personal Seizure Tracking Journal
The Ultimate Boogeyman Safari: A Journey into the Boogie World and Beyond
Whispers of Samhain: 1,000 Spells of Love, Luck, and Lunar Magic: Samhain Spell Book
Apophis's guides:
Witch's Spellbook Crafting Guide for Halloween
Frost & Flame: The Enchanted Yule Grimoire of 1000 Winter Spells
The Ultimate Boogey Goo Guide & Spooky Activities for Halloween Fun
Harmony of the Scales: A Libra's Spellcraft for Balance and Beauty
The Enchanted Advent: 36 Days of Christmas Wonders

Nightmare Mansion: The Labyrinth of Screams
Harvest of Enchantment: 1,000 Spells of Gratitude, Love, and Fortune for Thanksgiving
The Boogey Chronicles: A Journal of Nightly Encounters and Shadowy Secrets
The 12 Days of Financial Freedom: A Step-by-Step Christmas Countdown to Transform Your Finances
Sigil of the Eternal Spiral Blank Journal
A Christmas Feast: Timeless Recipes for Every Meal
Holiday Stress-Free Solutions: A Survival Guide to Thriving During the Festive Season
Yu-Gi-Oh! Holiday Gifting Mastery: The Ultimate Guide for Fans and Newcomers Alike
Holiday Harmony: A Hydrocephalus Survival Guide for the Festive Season
Celestial Craft: The Witch's Almanac for 2025 – A Cosmic Guide to Manifestations, Moons, and Mystical Events
Doctor Who: The Toymaker's Winter Wonderland
Tulsa King Unveiled: A Thrilling Guide to Stallone's Mafia Masterpiece
Pendulum Craft: A Complete Guide to Crafting and Using Personalized Divination Tools
Nightmare Mansion: Santa's Eternal Eve
Starlight Noel: A Cosmic Journey through Christmas Mysteries
The Dark Architect: Unlocking the Blueprint of Existence
Surviving the Embrace: The Ultimate Guide to Encounters with The Hugging Molly
The Enchanted Codex: Secrets of the Craft for Witches, Wiccans, and Pagans
Harvest of Gratitude: A Complete Thanksgiving Guide

Yuletide Essentials: A Complete Guide to an Authentic and Magical Christmas
Celestial Smokes: A Cosmic Guide to Cigars and Astrology
Living in Balance: A Comprehensive Survival Guide to Thriving with Diabetes Insipidus
Cosmic Symbiosis: The Venom Zodiac Chronicles
The Cursed Paw of Ambition
Cosmic Symbiosis: The Astrological Venom Journal
Celestial Wonders Unfold: A Stargazer's Guide to the Cosmos (2024-2029)
The Ultimate Black Friday Prepper's Guide: Mastering Shopping Strategies and Savings
Cosmic Sales: The Astrological Guide to Black Friday Shopping
Legends of the Corn Mother and Other Harvest Myths
Whispers of the Harvest: The Corn Mother's Journal
The Evergreen Spellbook
The Doctor Meets the Boogeyman
The White Witch of Rose Hall's SpellBook
The Gingerbread Golem's Shadow: A Study in Sweet Darkness
The Gingerbread Golem Codex: An Academic Exploration of Sweet Myths
The Gingerbread Golem Grimoire: Sweet Magicks and Spells for the Festive Witch
The Curse of the Gingerbread Golem
10-minute Christmas Crafts for kids
Christmas Crisis Solutions: The Ultimate Last-Minute Survival Guide
Gingerbread Golem Recipes: Holiday Treats with a Magical Twist
The Infinite Key: Unlocking Mystical Secrets of the Ages
Enchanted Yule: A Wiccan and Pagan Guide to a Magical and Memorable Season
Dinosaurs of Power: Unlocking Ancient Magick
Astro-Dinos: The Cosmic Guide to Prehistoric Wisdom
Gallifrey's Yule Logs: A Festive Doctor Who Cookbook
The Dino Grimoire: Secrets of Prehistoric Magick
The Gift They Never Knew They Needed
The Gingerbread Golem's Culinary Alchemy: Enchanting Recipes for a Sweetly Dark Feast
A Time Lord Christmas: Holiday Adventures with the Doctor
Krampusproofing Your Home: Defensive Strategies for Yule
Silent Frights: A Collection of Christmas Creepypastas to Chill Your Bones
Santa Raptor's Jolly Carnage: A Dino-Claus Christmas Tale
Prehistoric Palettes: A Dino Wicca Coloring Journey
The Christmas Wishkeeper Chronicles
The Starlight Sleigh: A Holiday Journey
Elf Secrets: The True Magic of the North Pole
Candy Cane Conjurations
Cooking with Kids: Recipes Under 20 Minutes
Doctor Who: The TARDIS Confiscation
The Anxiety First Aid Kit: Quick Tools to Calm Your Mind

Frosty Whispers: A Winter's Tale
The Infinite Key: Unlocking the Secrets to Prosperity, Resilience, and Purpose
The Grasping Void: Why You'll Regret This Purchase
Astrology for Busy Bees: Star Signs Simplified
The Instant Focus Formula: Cut Through the Noise
The Secret Language of Colors: Unlocking the Emotional Codes
Sacred Fossil Chronicles: Blank Journal
The Christmas Cottage Miracle
Feeding Frenzy: Graboid-Inspired Recipes
Manifest in Minutes: The Quick Law of Attraction Guide
The Symbiote Chronicles: Doctor Who's Venomous Journey
Think Tiny, Grow Big: The Minimalist Mindset
The Energy Key: Unlocking Limitless Motivation
New Year, New Magic: Manifesting Your Best Year Yet
Unstoppable You: Mastering Confidence in Minutes
Infinite Energy: The Secret to Never Feeling Drained
Lightning Focus: Mastering the Art of Productivity in a Distracted World
Saturnalia Manifestation Magick: A Guide to Unlocking Abundance During the Solstice
Graboids and Garland: The Ultimate Tremors-Themed Christmas Guide
12 Nights of Holiday Magic
The Power of Pause: 60-Second Mindfulness Practices
The Quick Reset: How to Reclaim Your Life After Burnout
The Shadow Eater: A Tale of Despair and Survival
The Micro-Mastery Method: Transform Your Skills in Just Minutes a Day
Reclaiming Time: How to Live More by Doing Less
Chronovore: The Eternal Nexus
The Mind Reset: Unlocking Your Inner Peace in a Chaotic World
Confidence Code: Building Unshakable Self-Belief
Baby the Vampire Terrier
Baby the Vampire Terrier's Christmas Adventure
Celestial Streams: The Content Creator's Astrology Manual
The Wealth Whisperer: Unlocking Abundance with Everyday Actions
The Energy Equation: Maximize Your Output Without Burning Out
The Happiness Algorithm: Science-Backed Steps to Joyful Living
Stress-Free Success: Achieving Goals Without Anxiety
Mindful Wealth: The New Blueprint for Financial Freedom
The Festive Flavors of New Year: A Culinary Celebration
The Master's Gambit: Keys of Eternal Power
Shadowed Secrets: Groundhog Day Mysteries
Beneath the Burrow: Lessons from the Groundhog
Spring's Whispers: The Groundhog's Prediction

The Limitless Mindset: Unlock Your Untapped Potential
The Focus Funnel: How to Cut Through Chaos and Get Results
Bold Moves: Building Courage to Live on Your Terms
The Daily Shift: Simple Practices for Lasting Transformation
The Quarter-Life Reset: Thriving in Your 20s and 30s
The Art of Shadowplay: Building Your Own Personal Myth
The Eternal Loop: Finding Purpose in Repetition
Burrowing Wisdom: Life Lessons from the Groundhog
Shadow Work: A Groundhog Day Perspective
Love in Bloom: 5-Minute Romantic Gestures
The Shadowspell Codex: Secrets of Forbidden Magick
The Burnout Cure: Finding Balance in a Busy World
The Groundhog Prophecy: Unlocking Seasonal Secrets
Nog Tales: The Spirited History of Eggnog
Six More Weeks: Embracing Seasonal Transitions
The Lumivian Chronicles: Fragments of the Fifth Dimension
Money on Your Mind: A Beginner's Guide to Wealth
The Focus Fix: Breaking Through Distraction
January's Spirit Keepers: Mystical Protectors of the Cold
Creativity Unchained: Unlocking Your Wildest Ideas in 2025
Manifestation Mastery: 365 Days to Rewrite Your Reality
The Groundhog's Mirror: Reflecting on Change
The Weeping Angels' Christmas Curse
Burrowed in Time: A Groundhog Day Journey
Heartbeats: Poems to Share with Your Valentine
Dino Wicca: The Sacred Grimoire of Prehistoric Magick
Courage of the Pride: Finding Your Inner Roar
The Lion's Leap: Bold Moves for Big Results
Healthy Hustle: Achieving Without Overworking
Practical Manifesting: Turning Dreams into Reality in 2025
Jurassic Pharaohs: Unlocking the Magick of Ancient Egypt and Dino Wicca
The Happiness Equation: Small Changes for Big Joy
The Confidence Compass: Finding Your Inner Strength
Whispers in the Hollow: Tales of the Forgotten Beasts
Echoes from the Hollow: The Return of Forgotten Beasts
The Hollow Ascendant: The Rise of the Forgotten Beasts
The Relationship Reset: Building Better Connections
Mastering the Morning: How to Win the Day Before 8 AM
The Shadow's Dance: Groundhog Day Symbolism
Cupid's Kitchen: Quick Valentine's Day Recipes
Valentine's Day on a Budget: Love Without Breaking the Bank

Astrocraft: Aligning the Stars in the World of Minecraft
Forecasting Life: Groundhog Day Reflections
Bleeding Hearts: Twisted Tales of Valentine's Terror
Herbal Smoke Revolution: The Ultimate Guide to Nature's Cigarette Alternative
Winter's Wrath: The Complete Survival Blueprint for Extreme Freezes.
The Groundhog's Shadow: A Tale of Seasons
Burrowed Insights: Wisdom from the Groundhog
Sensual Strings: The Art of Erotic Bondage
Whispered Flames: Unlocking the Power of Fire Play
Forgotten Shadows: A Guide to Cryptids Lost to Time
Six Weeks of Secrets: Groundhog Day's Hidden Messages
Shadows and Cycles: Groundhog Day Reflections
The Art of Love Letters: Crafting the Perfect Message
Romantic Getaways at Home: Turning Your Space into Paradise
Purrfect Brews: A Cat Lover's Guide to Coffee and Companionship
The Groundhog's Wisdom: Timeless Lessons for Modern Life
The Shadow Oracle: Groundhog Day as a Predictor
Emerging from the Burrow: A Journey of Renewal
The Language of Love: Learning Your Partner's Love Style
Authorpreneur: The Ultimate Blueprint for Writing, Publishing, and Thriving as an Author
Weathering the Seasons: Groundhog Day Perspectives
Valentine's Day Magic: A Guide to Romantic Rituals
The Shadow Chronicles: Stories of Groundhog Day
Love and Laughter: Fun Games for Valentine's Day
AstroRealty: Unlocking the Stars for Property Success
The Groundhog's Path: A Guide to Seasonal Balance
Groundhog Day Diaries: Reflections in the Shadow
The Groundhog's Light: Illuminating the Path Ahead
Valentine's Traditions from Around the World

If you want solar for your home go here: https://www.harborsolar.live/apophisenterprises/

Get Some Tarot cards: https://www.makeplayingcards.com/sell/apophis-occult-shop

Get some shirts: https://www.bonfire.com/store/apophis-shirt-emporium/

Instagrams:
@apophis_enterprises,
@apophisbookemporium,
@apophisscardshop
Twitter: @apophisenterpr1
Tiktok:@apophisenterprise
Youtube: @sg1fan23477, @FiresideRetreatKingdom
Hive: @sg1fan23477
CheeLee: @SG1fan23477

Podcast: Apophis Chat Zone: https://open.spotify.com/show/5zXbr-CLEV2xzCp8ybrfHsk?si=fb4d4fdbdce44dec

Newsletter: https://apophiss-newsletter-27c897.beehiiv.com/

If you want to support me or see posts of other projects that I have come over to: **buymeacoffee.com/mpetchinskg**

I post there daily several times a day

Get your Dinowicca or Christmas themed digital products, especially Santa Raptor songs and other musics. Here: **https://sg1fan23477.gumroad.com**

Apophis Yuletide Digital has not only digital Christmas items, but it will have all things with Dinowicca as well as other Digital products.

www.ingramcontent.com/pod-product-compliance
Lightning Source LLC
LaVergne TN
LVHW060036210926
848481LV00013B/3879
* 9 7 9 8 3 4 8 4 5 8 7 0 6 *